THE INFLUENCE OF THE LATIN ELEGISTS

on

English Lyric Poetry, 1600-1650

with Particular Reference to

THE WORKS OF

ROBERT HERRICK

———•———

By

PAULINE AIKEN

---•---

Phaeton Press

New York

1970

Originally Published 1932
Reprinted 1970

Library of Congress Catalog Card Number — 78-91345
Published by PHAETON PRESS, INC.
SBN 87753-002-5

To

JOHN W. DRAPER

PREFACE

The subject of the influence of the Latin elegiac poets upon English lyric poetry of the seventeenth century prior to the Restoration was suggested to me in 1927 by Dr. John W. Draper. The problem has necessitated some familiarity with the works of the Elegists, and the reading of all available lyric poetry published between 1600 and 1660. The method of presentation adopted has required somewhat extended quotations both of English poems and of Latin parallels. The results indicate an undoubted influence of the Latin Elegists upon seventeenth century English poetry, particularly upon the verse of Robert Herrick.

The reading for this thesis was done chiefly at the Widener Library of Harvard University. I have also used the Bangor Public Library and the Library of the University of Maine.

I am deeply indebted to Dean George Davis Chase, to whose profound knowledge of Latin literature I owe whatever understanding I have of the Elegists, and without whose friendly interest and guidance I should have had the greatest difficulty in dealing with the Latin phases of my subject. My thanks are also due to Dr. Milton Ellis, who, during the absence of Dr. Draper, directed the first year's work upon this thesis. To Dr. John W. Draper, the director of this thesis, whose stimulating guidance and unfailing kindness have made possible the completion of this work, I particularly wish to express my sincere appreciation.

Pauline Aiken

Orono, Maine
September, 1931

TABLE OF CONTENTS

Page

Preface 5

Introduction 9

Chapter   I.   The Latin Love Elegy 11

Chapter   II.   Elegiac Influences on

the "Three Schools" 27

Chapter III.   Elegiac Themes in Herrick's Verse 48

Chapter IV.   Herrick's Love Poetry 84

Conclusion 106

Bibliography 109

Index 111

INTRODUCTION

Likenesses between the Latin elegists of the Augustan age and the English lyrists of the seventeenth century are easily recognizable. Many Cavalier writers expressly mention the Roman poets, and certain of the Augustan love pieces have been paraphrased by several members of the English school. The spirit and tone of the two groups are very similar. The whole tradition of a series of love poems addressed to a mistress is common to both. Much of their subject matter also is the same. The complaints on a mistress' cruelty, the ecstasies upon enjoying her favors, and the glorifying of the most trivial details of her daily life are the stock themes of both. The poetry of each group is artificial and sophisticated. In both appears the tendency to write, as mere literary exercises, series of poems embodying a set tradition of love. Both abound in witty gallantries and exaggerated flattery; both are frank, often to the point of indecency; both indulge at times in bitter and most unchivalrous recriminations. In short, it is evident that the two groups, tho separated by some seventeen hundred years, are governed by literary traditions of striking similarity.

In spite of these obvious resemblances, however, the subject of the influence of the ancient upon the modern group has never been adequately investigated. K. F. Smith in his edition of Tibullus[1] notes his author's influence on various Continental writers, and remarks that echoes of Tibullus may be traced in Daniel, Cowley, Rowe, Walsh, and others, and that there is some analogy between Tibullus and Herrick. He contends, however, that Herrick did not imitate the Latin poet. He gives no definite references: Professor Smith, in *Illustrations on Tibullus*,[2] remarks influences on Continental writers, but merely glances at the echoes in English poets. Professor Robinson Ellis in his works on Catullus[3] does not discuss the poet's influence on modern English literature. K. P. Harrington's book on Catullus[4] does note specific influences,

---

[1]Smith, Kirby Flower, *The Works of Albius Tibullus*, pp. 62 *et seq.*

[2]Smith, Kirby Flower, *Illustrations on Tibullus*, Am. Jour. Phil. XLIII, pp. 49-54.

[3]Ellis, Robinson, *Commentary on Catullus, Prolegomena*, and *Catullus in the Fourteenth Century*.

[4]Harrington, K. P., *Catullus and His Influence*, pp. 157 *et seq.*

but Catullus is not one of the major Elegists. E. K. Rand's work on Ovid[5] does not give specific examples. A. C. Judson's collection of seventeenth century lyrics[6] occasionally notes echoes of definite passages from the Elegists, but the volume is a slender one—a slight fragment of the mass of Cavalier poetry. F. W. Moorman, in *The Cambridge History of English Literature,* suggests influences of Ovid and Catullus, but does not go into details. Duff's study of Latin literature[7] notes analogies between Herrick and Catullus, but does not continue with the topic. In short, there are numerous references to the subject, but no real investigation of it.

The scope of the present work is limited to the influence of the Augustan erotic elegy upon English non-religious and non-dramatic poetry during the period 1600 to 1650. Ovid's elegiac *Ars Amatoria* and *Remedia Amoris,* on account of their specialized theme and purpose, do not, strictly speaking, fall within the traditions of the love elegy, and for this reason are excluded from this study. On the other hand, certain of Catullus' hendecasyllabic love poems, because of their close resemblance in subject and spirit to the true elegy, have been included.

It has seemed wise to prefix to the main body of this study a discussion of the origin of the elegy and of the works of the major poets whose influence is to be considered. These topics, accordingly, will be the subject of the first chapter.

---

[5]Rand, E. K., *Ovid and His Influence.*
[6]Judson, A. C., *Seventeenth Century Lyrics.*
[7]Duff, J. W., *A Literary History of Rome,* pp. 327-328.

CHAPTER I

THE LATIN LOVE ELEGY

The Latin love elegy, like practically all other forms of Latin literature, did not originate with the Romans. It was, in fact, even further removed from its sources than most other forms of Roman literary art. It was an imitation of an imitation, its models being the artificial and imitative love poems of the decadent Alexandrine school. But tho these direct models of the Roman elegy were late Greek, the type of poetry to which they belonged was far from being a recent invention. It was, in fact, a very ancient and venerable type, second in antiquity only to the epic, and dating back to the eighth century before Christ.

The beginnings of the elegy are found in the Ionian colonies of Asia Minor.[8] Here, as early as 750 B.C., it was customary to sing, at the burial of the dead, songs of lament accompanied by the flute. These songs appear to have been chiefly in hexameters, and had a set refrain of lamentation: ἒ λέγε ἒ λέγε ἒ. From this refrain the Greeks derived the name of the meter ἐλεγεῖον (sc. μέτρον), and called a poem written in the metre τά ἐλεγεῖα, later ἡ ἐλεγεία (sc. Ποίησις).[9] Unfortunately, the etymology of the refrain is very uncertain.[10]

Besides giving a name to the type of verse, the refrain ἒ λέγε ἒ λέγε ἒ determined the metre of the elegy.[11] Doubled, it forms the so-called pentameter line, which in elegiac metre alternates with the hexameter. The flowing hexameter line was narrative, while the pentameter with its syncopation was reflective and had the effect

---

[8]Schulze, Dr. K. P., *Römische Elegiker, Eine Auswahl aus Catull, Tibull, Properz, und Ovid*, p. 3.

[9]Schulze, *op. cit.*, p. 3.

[10]*The Century Dictionary* states that it is Greek: "Cry woe, cry woe, woe!" According to Croiset, ἔλεγος (derived from ἒ λέγε) appears to have meant originally a flute of reed-cane, and is from an Asiatic language. According to Harper's *Dictionary of Classical Literature and Antiquities*, ἔλεγος is probably not Greek but Lydian, and means a plaintive melody accompanied by the flute.

[11]Schanz, Martin, *Geschicte der Römischen Litteratur bis zum Gesetzgebungswerk des Kaisers Justinian.*

of a minor chord. The standard illustration of the metre in English is Coleridge's translation of Schiller's couplet :[12]

> In the hexameter rises the fountain's silvery column,
> In the pentameter aye falling in melody back.

Both in form and in historical development the elegy is half way between the epic and the lyric.[13] In form, it has a hexameter line, the ordinary vehicle of epic narrative, plus a peculiar form of pentameter verse which is particularly suited to expressing emotion—the province of the true lyric. Chronologically, moreover, the development of the elegy follows the epic and precedes the lyric.

The earliest elegy, then, was a funereal song using a hexameter line, probably in praise of the deceased, followed by a set pentameter refrain of lamentation, usually accompanied by the flute. This conception, however, soon broadened. The fixed refrain was replaced by a verse metrically the same. By the seventh century before Christ the elegy had come to be used to express not merely lamentation, but all kinds of personal reflections. It was now frequently recited at festivals. It had discarded accompaniment, and was read, not sung.[14]

The oldest preserved elegy was written by Callinus of Ephesus (fl. c. 700 B.C.). With him this type had already progressed far beyond the narrow limits of its original meaning. His elegies were political poems, chiefly calls to war. By them he summoned his countrymen against the Cimmerian hordes who were raiding Asia Minor.[15] The second known elegist was Tyrtaeus, the lame schoolmaster of Athens. The songs by which he encouraged the Spartans against the Messenians were, in part at least, elegies. Archilochus of Paros, who is said to have invented the iambic foot, also wrote elegiac verse.[16]

---

[12]"Im Hexameter steigt des Springquells flüssige Säule,
    Im Pentameter drauf fällt sie melodisch herab."
                                    Schiller, *Gedichte,* "Das Distichon."
[13]Schulze, *op. cit.,* p. 4.
[14]Croiset, Alfred and Maurice, *Abridged History of Greek Literature,* p. 89.
[15]Schulze, *op. cit.,* p. 4.
[16]Croiset, *op. cit.,* p. 94.

Solon of Athens (c. 639-559 B.C.) marks another step in the development of the elegy. He used it, not as a call to arms, but to express political and ethical maxims. Other writers of the γνῶμαι, or gnomic elegies, were Xenophanes of Colophon (founder of the Eleatic school of philosophy), Theognis of Megara, and Phocylides of Miletus.[17]

In spite of the success of the elegy as a political form, the ancients appear to have realized very early that it was better adapted to expressing subjective feeling. About 600 B.C., Mimnermus of Colophon[18] wrote a series of elegies in praise of love to his sweetheart, Nanno. He used traces of narrative to illustrate his theme, but the main point was love;[19] and thus he became the founder of the erotic elegy. About 500 B.C., Simonides of Ceos wrote elegiac laments for the Athenian soldiers who fell in the Persian War. It was he who composed the famous epitaph of Leonidas. Thereafter the elegy was employed almost entirely for the expression of emotion—sometimes joy but more often sorrow—and especially, the motifs of Mimnermus and Simonides blending into a composite theme, the elegy came to express the sorrows of love.

The erotic elegy continued to be written. About 400 B.C., Antimachus of Colophon,[20] a friend of Plato, sought to console himself for the death of his beloved Lyde by recounting at wearying length similar woes in the lives of legendary heroes. The mythological element was made an independent factor, merely bound together by his own feeling,[21] and became a pattern for the Alexandrians. With Antimachus we have the beginning of the learned erotic elegy.

The elegy was soon to be translated to a new center. Alexandria was founded, and very early began to rise to notice as a literary and scholastic center. Around the great museum and libraries established by the Ptolemies was developing the most learned and cultivated society of ancient times. Breasted states

[17]Schulze, *op. cit.*, p. 5.
[18]Croiset, *op. cit.*, p. 100.
[19]"Plus in amore valet Mimnermi versus Homero."
      Propertius, I, ix, 11.
[20]Schulze, *op. cit.*, p. 5.
[21]Schanz, *op. cit.*

that, in numbers, wealth, commerce, power, and in all the arts of civilization, Alexandria was now the greatest city of the whole ancient world.[22]   Greek, Asiatic, and Egyptian fused their tastes into a composite of learning, profusion, and sensuality.   Social as well as intellectual life flourished here in an atmosphere of learned leisure.   In society, women played an important role.   It was a city made up of men of many racial stocks; hence it lacked the narrowness of a purely national viewpoint.   Wealth and culture and scholarship fused in this great cosmopolitan city into a society brilliant and sophisticated, learned and very conscious of its learning.   It is in this setting that the next act in the development of the elegy is to take place.

The literature of Alexandria mirrored her civilization.   It was highly wrought, ornate, very artificial—poetry by the learned for the learned.[23]   The social importance of women is indicated by the amount of verse addressed to them; such poetry was usually amorous; much of it sensuous to the point of being vile.   Aside from sensuality, the chief faults of Alexandrian verse were pedantry and over-elaboration.   Writers were fond of showing their erudition by referring to gods, heroes, etc., by as many different epithets as possible.   They particularly delighted in obscure patronymics and geographical allusions.   They constantly turned back to old legends of gods and heroes, and inserted their amorous adventures in poem after poem—not because of religious enthusiasm or patriotic admiration, but simply as learned decorations for their themes.   In the words of Duff: "Mythology had become machinery, and love gallantry."[24]

The elegy in Alexandria developed along very definite lines, and was a favorite form.   It abandoned the last vestiges of its old-time scope and became preëminently the poetry of love.   The plaintive pentameter was equally applicable to funeral dirge and love's lament.   To quote W. Y. Sellar:

> The Alexandrians not only revived the use of the elegiac metre, largely employed for the expression of personal feelings in the earlier era of Greek poetry, but formed elegiac poetry into a new branch of literary art.... The motive of this poetry was the sentiment and pas-

---

[22]Breasted, James Henry, *Ancient Times*, p. 461.
[23]Duff, J. Wight, *A Literary History of Rome*, p. 306.
[24]*Ibid.*

sion, the pleasure and the pain of love. The substance was largely drawn from actual life, but the romance of older love stories....was revived to glorify the realism of the present.[25]

The Alexandrian elegy, so far as can be judged from its remaining fragments and from the Roman love lyrics based upon it, conformed to the original idea of the elegy, and bore to a large extent the character of a *querimonia,* either a complaint of the cruelty of a mistress or a mere expression of the "luxury of melancholy."[26] The Alexandrians wrote both subjective and objective love elegies —i.e., poems describing their own experiences and those describing the love affairs of others, usually of mythological heroes. In both forms the erotic elegy reached Rome.[27]

The first in date of the Alexandrian elegists was Philetas, born at Cos about 340 B.C. He was a grammarian and teacher as well as a poet—*doctus* and *poeta.* His chief elegiac work is the Παίγνια, a collection of amorous verse about his sweetheart, Bittis. Only about fifty lines of his works remain, so that it is chiefly by the praises of his successors that we may judge his greatness.[28] He followed Antimachus of Colophon in that he included mythology and love in his elegies; but whereas the earlier poet used the mythology as a separate element, Philetas blended it closely with his love confessions, thus setting the type for the Alexandrian elegy. Of his principal followers it is sufficient to mention Hermesianax of Colophon, Phanocles, and Alexander of Aetolia. The first mentioned of the three wrote such light and elegant verse that it is recorded by one of the ancients that he had to wear shoes with leaden soles to keep from being blown away.[29] He wrote three books of elegies, entitled *Leontium,* from the name of his mistress.[30] A long fragment of the third book is preserved, and is a typical example of the Alexandrian elegy—sensuous, polished, and pedantic.

The Alexandrian who most influenced the Romans was Callimachus. He, like Philetas, was both grammarian and poet.

---

[25]Sellar, W. Y., *The Roman Poets of the Augustan Age,* pp. 205-206.
[26]*Ibid.,* p. 206.
[27]Schanz, *op. cit.*
[28]Croiset, *op. cit.,* p. 441.
[29]Sandys, John Edwin, *History of Classical Scholarship,* p. 118 and note 6.
[30]Croiset, *op. cit.,* p. 441.

His motto was "Small but fine." Instead of introducing the woes of many heroes, he treats a single saga in great detail and with much learning. He narrates, but the narrative in his poems is not their chief point. Often he recounts only the very climax of the action, and makes that a mere pivot upon which to hang the love element.[31]

Callimachus was particularly admired and imitated by the Romans. His Αἴτια (*Causes* or *Origins*), a learned collection of Greek legends dealing with the origin of certain cities, families, or customs, was imitated by Propertius in his *Origines,* and the idea of Ovid's *Fasti* seems to be drawn from the same work. His *Lock of Berenice* was translated by Catullus. Ovid imitated his *Ibis,* and mentions him after Homer and Hesiod and along with Sophocles and Menander among the poets whose words will live forever;[32] and Quintilian ranks him first among the Greek elegists, placing Philetas second.[33]

In the year 73 B.C., the Alexandrian elegy came into direct contact with Rome, when Parthenius of Nicea,[34] one of the last of the Alexandrian poets, was taken prisoner in the Mithridatic war and brought to Rome. Here he became the teacher of Gallus, thus uniting the Greek and Roman elegy.

The Alexandrian elegy was peculiarly fitted to Rome at this period.[35] The growth of critical studies had helped to elevate Greek literature to the heights and to depress the native Latin verse. Whereas the earlier Latin poets had imitated Greek epic or drama, the poets of the Augustan age were for the most part too subjective, too self-centered for the epic and not bold enough to undertake it. On the other hand, they were too practical for the pure lyric, too self-conscious for inspiration.[36] The Alexandrian elegy, then, with its combination of narrative and emotion, was peculiarly fitted to the tastes and capacities of the time. It was not too pretentious to be easily imitated. Its highly wrought form

---

[31]Schanz, *op. cit.*
[32]Ovid, *Amores* I, xv, 1. 13:
Battiades semper toto cantabitur orbe.
[33]Sellar, *op. cit.,* p. 205.
[34]Schulze, *op. cit.,* p. 6.
[35]Duff, *op. cit.,* p. 303.
[36]Schulze, *op. cit.,* p. 7.

appealed to the fastidious Roman taste. Its elaboration of detail, its mass of learned allusion pleased a Rome that had learned, largely from the Alexandrians themselves, to love minute points of scholarship and obscure mythological details.

Moreover, socially and politically the age had come more and more to resemble the epoch of Alexandria's supremacy. Rome was, as Alexandria had been, the center of the civilized world. The time was an age of peace following a period of war, a time of revulsion from strife and bloodshed. Society was again brilliant, cultured, and artificial. Literary patronage was practised and encouraged by the Emperor himself. Women were once more socially prominent. It was, then, entirely natural that the fashionable movement in poetry should be "to carry to their perfection the Alexandrian tendencies."[37]

The chief marks of the school at Rome were "assiduous translation, study of versification, prizing of rarities in phrase, avoidance of long works, and disdain for the old Latin poetry."[38] Apart from spirit, its influence consisted in "intensified care for form, in fixed ordinances regulating metrical quantity, and in the rescue of the final -*s* which earlier poets had elided."[39]

Latin elegiac verse had been written before the Augustan period. Ennius had used it, as the early Greeks had, for epigrams and inscriptions. Lucilius employed it in one book of satires. Early in the first century B.C., Quintus Catullus and Valerius Aedituus used it for short erotic pieces. Catullus, however, was the first Roman to make wide and varied use of the metre. He used it for both bitter and tender love poems, in short satiric pieces, and in two beautiful poems of lamentation for the death of his brother.[40]

The Augustans, then, were not the first Roman elegists; and the points which distinguish them from the earlier Roman poets are, first, perfection of the metre and, second, the definite giving over to the elegy of the province of love poetry.[41] They improved upon the Alexandrians: first, in that they to some extent, at least, freed the elegy from its burden of pedantic learning; second, as

---

[37]Sellar, *op. cit.*, p. 211.
[38]Duff, *op. cit.*, p. 306.
[39]*Ibid.*, p. 307.
[40]Sellar, *op. cit.*, pp. 206-207.
[41]Duff, *op. cit.*, p. 548.

a result of this, they achieved a freshness and energy new to the erotic elegy. In other words, the older Romans were influenced by the Ionian Greeks. Both wrote elegies in the broader sense of the word—i.e., their verses might be on any theme, so long as they were elegiac in metre. The Augustans, on the other hand, imitated the narrower Alexandrian elegies both in subject and form. Sellar says: "They nationalized the Alexandrian elegy of Philetas and Callimachus as Virgil had nationalized the Sicilian pastoral of Theocritus."[42]

There were many poets of love in the Augustan period, but the ancients included in the list of genuine elegiac poets only four: Gallus, Tibullus, Propertius, and Ovid.[43] Ovid himself was the first to make this list, and Quintilian keeps it unchanged. Even Catullus is omitted, for tho he wrote elegiac verse, it forms only a small part of his work, and his greatest poems are in other metres.

Of the works of Gallus, the first poet on the list, little is known. His poems have entirely disappeared. We know that he was a friend of Virgil, who admired his poetic gifts. It has been conjectured that he wrote the *Ciris*. His works were an adaptation of one of Euphorion's poems, and four books of elegies on Lycoris (the actress Cytheris, a mistress of Mark Antony). Our only information as to his style is that Quintilian says he was *"durior"* than his successors.[44]

One poet whom the ancients did not include in their list of Elegists must be mentioned here. Catullus, tho the bulk of his work is not elegiac, yet made varied and effective use of the metre. *Carmina* LXV thru CXVI are elegies. They include his *Lock of Berenice,* translated from Callimachus (No. LXVI), two beautiful songs of lamentation for the death of his brother (Nos. LXV and CI), a poem expressing thanks to a friend for access to a house where the poet may meet his mistress, many bitter satiric epigrams, and a number of brief erotic pieces. The latter include some of his finest work.

Moreover, much of Catullus' hendecasyllabic verse is in the tradition of the love elegy. Like the other poets of the erotic school, he addresses most of his verse to a mistress. She is the

---

[42]Sellar, *op. cit.,* p. 208.

[43]*Ibid.,* p. 209.

[44]Duff, *op. cit.,* pp. 550-551.

beautiful and unscrupulous Clodia, wife of Metellus Celer, governor of Cisalpine Gaul. Following the traditions of love poetry, Catullus addresses her by a name metrically equivalent to her own. He calls her Lesbia, a name reminiscent of the Lesbian poetess, Sappho.[45] All his poems to her reflect the spirit of the erotic elegy, tho some of the most famous ones are in the eleven syllabled metre. For example, the much imitated

> Vivamus mea Lesbia atque amemus

parallels in spirit and phraseology elegies of Propertius and Tibullus. Compare:

> Vivamus mea Lesbia atque amemus.
> soles occidere et redire possunt:
> nobis cum semel occidit brevis lux,
> nox est perpetua una dormienda.[46]

with

> Quare, dum licet, inter nos laetemur amantes:
> non satis est ullo tempore longus amor.[47]

A still closer parallel is

> Dum nos fata sinunt, oculos satiemus amore:
> nox tibi longa venit, nec reditura dies.[48]

In similar mood Tibullus sings

> Interea, dum fata sinunt, iungamus amores;[49]

and again

> At si tardus eris, errabis. Transiit aetas
> quam cito! Non segnis stat remeatve dies.[50]

Among other parallels between Catullus' hendecasyllables and the elegies of Tibullus, Propertius, and Ovid may be noted the farewells to love of three of the poets:

---

[45]Duff, *op. cit.*, p. 313.
[46]Catullus, V, ll. 3-6.
[47]Propertius, I, xiv, ll. 25-26.
[48]Propertius, II, xv, ll. 23-24.
[49]Tibullus, I, i, l. 69.
[50]Tibullus, I, iv, ll. 27-28.

> Sed obstinata mente perfer, obdura.
> Vale puella. Iam Catullus obdurat.[51]
>
> Vicimus et domitum pedibus calcamus amorem, ...
> perfer et obdura: dolor hic tibi proderit olim.[52]
>
> Dum licet,　iniusto subtrahe colla iugo.
> Nec tu non aliquid, sed prima nocte dolebis;
> omne in amore malum, si patiare, leve est.[53]

Both Catullus and the Elegists proper sing the praises of wine, as in the following passages:

> Minister vetuli puer　Falerni
> inger mi calices amariores. . . .
> at vos quolubet hinc abite, lymphae,
> vini pernicies, et ad severos
> migrate.[54]
>
> Care puer, madeant generoso pocula baccho,
> et nobis prona funde Falerna manu.[55]
>
> Largius effuso madeat tibi mensa Falerno,
> spumet et aurato mollius in calice.[56]

This community of subject matter, diction, and spirit, added to the fact that Catullus used the elegiac metre for some of the best of his love poems, links the poet so closely to the school of the Elegists that it has seemed advisable to include in the present work the influence of his love songs in hendecasyllables as well as his true elegies.

Tibullus, the second on Ovid's list, is the least Alexandrian of Roman elegists.[57] His poems are marked by greater simplicity in theme, diction, and tone than can be found in the works of the other poets of the group. He writes almost entirely on four themes: country life, praise of Messala (his patron), the ancient

---

[51]Catullus, VIII, ll. 11-12.
[52]Ovid, *Amores,* III, xxi a, ll. 5 and 7.
[53]Propertius, II, v, ll. 14-16.
[54]Catullus, XXVII, ll. 1-2 and 5-7.
[55]Tibullus, III, vi, ll. 5-6.
[56]Pro. II, xxxiii, ll. 39-40.
[57]Duff, *op. cit.,* p. 547.

religious rites and festivals of the country folk, and, above all, love.[58] These four themes he blends and varies with admirable skill. Some of his poems· contain all four. Note, for example, the first elegy of Book II :

> Quisque adest, faveat : fruges lustramus et agros,
> ritus ut a prisco traditus extat avo.[59]

and

> ... Messala ...
> huc ades aspiraque mihi, dum carmine nostro
> redditur agricolis gratia caelitibus.
> rura cano rurisque deos.[60]
>
> A miseri, quos hic graviter deus urget! at ille
> felix, cui placidus leniter adflat Amor.[61]

His idea of happiness is life on a farm with his beloved beside him —a quiet idyllic existence varied only by the religious celebrations of the devout rustics and by an occasional visit from Messala.

> Rura colam, frugumque aderit mea Delia custos....
> huc veniet Mesalla meus cui dulcia poma
> Delia selectis detrahat arboribus.[62]

The true elegiac minor strain is recurringly present with Tibullus. A haunting fear of death obsesses him. Like the other elegists, he is acutely conscious of the fleetingness of youth and love ; and, more than they, he fears the darkness and loneliness of death.

> Interea, dum fata sinunt, iungamus amores,

he advises wistfully, for

> Iam veniet tenebris Mors adoperta caput.[63]

---

[58]Carter, Jesse Benedict, *Selections from the Roman Elegiac Poets,* Introduction, p. xxviii.

[59]Tib. II, i, ll. 1-2.

[60]Tib. II, i, ll. 35 *et seq.*.

[61]*Ibid.,* ll. 79-80.

[62]Tib. I, v, ll. 21 and 31-32.

[63]Tib. I, i, ll. 69-70.

Again, when sick in Phaeacia, he writes in terror

> Abstineas avidas Mors modo nigra manus;
> abstineas, Mors atra, precor.[61]

He has had enough experience in war to know the grimness of death. With gloomy fatalism he pictures his imagined fate:

> Nunc ad bella trahor, et iam quis forsitan hostis
> haesura in nostro tela gerit latere.[65]

"What madness to call black Death upon us by warfare!" he cries, and pictures vividly the horrors of the underworld:

> Quis furor est atram bellis accessere Mortem!
> Imminet et tacito clam venit illa pede.
> Non seges est infra, non vinea culta, sed audax
> Cerberus et Stygiae navita turpis aquae.
> Illic pertussisque genis ustoque capillo
> errat ad obscuros pallida turba lacus.[66]

Like the other Elegists, he sings first of all of love. He can be as tender as Catullus, as passionate as Propertius. In comparison with love, fame and wealth are nothing. Let the soldier, he says, be the cynosure of all eyes; let him be clad from head to foot in gold and silver, if only

> Ipse boves mea si tecum modo Delia possim
> iungere et in solito pascere monte pecus;
> et te dum liceat teneris retinere lacertis,
> mollis et inculta sit mihi somnus humo.[67]

The next poet in the group, Propertius, differs widely from Tibullus. He is avowedly the most Alexandrian of the Roman elegists. He styles himself the Roman Callimachus.[68] His poems are full of the learned mythological parallels and strained phrases of Alexandria. In both language and construction he constantly and consciously strives for effect. In intellect and imagination,

---

[61]Tib. I, iii, ll. 4-5.
[65]Tib. I, x, ll. 13-14.
[66]Tib. I, x, ll. 33-39.
[67]Tib. I, ii, ll. 71-75.
[68]Pro. IV, i, l. 64.

however, he is probably the greatest of the Roman elegists. If his lines become overweighted and crabbed, it is thru excess of thought and passion. His faults are those of a genius. His diction, tho obscure, is powerful, and his imagination, if strained at times, is lofty and splendid.

His mistress, whom he addresses as Cynthia, was Hostia, grand-daughter of the learned Hostius, author of a historical poem on the Illyrian War.[69] According to the poet's description, she was a stately beauty with auburn hair, slim, long hands, a fine form, and a gait like Juno's.

> Fulva coma est longaeque manus, et maxima toto
> corpore, et incedit vel Jove digna soror.[70]

Not only her great beauty, but her skill in playing and dancing, and the fact that she was a learned maid and a poetess held Propertius in thrall.

> Nec me tam facies, quamvis sit candida, cepit. . . .
> quantum quod posito formose saltat Iaccho,
>   egit ut euhantes dux Ariadna choros,
> et quantum, Aeolio cum temptat carmina plectro,
>   par Aganippeae ludere docta lyrae,
> et sua cum antiquae committit scripta Corinnae
>   carmina, quae quivis non putat aequa suis.[71]

Unfortunately Cynthia's moral qualities did not equal her physical and mental attractions, for her infidelities drove Propertius nearly mad. At one time he stayed away from her for a year. He still loved her, however, and after a partial reconciliation, in 25 B.C., he published under the title *Cynthia* the first book of his elegies. This volume not only won for its author admission into the circle of Maecenas, but sealed his reconciliation with his mistress,[72] who was talented enough to appreciate the worth of the poems she had inspired.

Tho the theme of nearly all his best work is love, Propertius' poems have a wide range of feeling and expression. The poet can

---

[69]Duff, *op. cit.*, pp. 362-363.
[70]Pro. II, ii, ll. 5-6.
[71]Pro. II, iii, ll. 9 and 17 *et seq.*
[72]Duff, *op. cit.*, pp. 563-7.

describe with boisterous humor how Cynthia routed her rivals
from a drinking party at his house;[73] he can pour out his heart
to her with a tenderness not excelled by Catullus at his best;[74] he

> qui caput et digitos et lumina nigra puellae
> et canat ut soleant molliter ire pedes?"

can crowd all her charm and capriciousness into a single beautiful,
trenchant line:

> Cynthia forma potens, Cynthia verba levis.[75]

He writes of love in all its phases—its passion, its tenderness, its
devotion, its fickleness, its quarrels and reconciliations, its joys,
and its bitterness. Whether his verse be mordant with cynicism
and grief or glowing with tenderest devotion, always it is passionate in intensity. Now he complains from the depths of wretched-
ness:

> Saepe ego multa tuae levitatis dura timebam,
>   hac tamen excepta, Cynthia, perfidia.[76]

again:

> Eripitur nobis iam pridem cara puella,....
> nullae sunt inimicitiae nisi amoris acerbae:
>   ipsum me iugula, lenior hostis ero;[77]

and again, with bitterness that approaches madness:

> Sic igitur prima moriere aetate, Properti?
>   Sed morere; interitu gaudeat illa tuo!
> Exagitet nostros Manes, sectetur et umbras,
>   insultetque rogis, calcet et ossa mea....
> sed non effugies: mecum moriaris oportet,
>   hoc eodem ferro stillet uterque cruor.[78]

Then, in joy as wild as his unhappiness has been, he cries:

---

[73]Pro. IV, viii, ll. 27 *et seq.*

[74]*E.g.* Pro. I, xix and II, xii, ll. 20-21: "If you slay me utterly," says
the poet, addressing Love, "where will you find one

[75]Pro. II, v, l. 28.

[76]Pro. I, xv, ll. 1-2.

[77]Pro. II, viii, ll. 1 and 3-4.

[78]Pro. II, viii a, ll. 17-21, 25-26.

... Cynthia rara mea est!
Nunc mihi summa licet contingere sidera plantis:
sive dies seu nox venerit, illa mea est![79]

Ovid, last of the great Roman elegists, is the most facile of the group. His verse is smoother and more highly polished than even that of Tibullus. He composed five works in erotic elegiac verse. In chronological order they are: the *Amores*,[80] the *Heroides,* the *Medicamina Faciei Femineae,* the *Ars Amatoria,* and the *Remedia Amoris.*[81] Of these, the *Amores* is a collection of true love elegies, and the *Heroides,* which is a group of letters from various legendary ladies to their lovers, contains the elements of love and complaint which are the basis of the elegy. The *Medicamina Faciei Femineae* is a treatise on the care of the complexion. The *Ars Amatoria* consists of three volumes of instructions on the art of provoking passion. The *Remedia Amoris,* a complement to the *Ars,* explains methods of stifling love. Only the first two works mentioned fall within the scope of this thesis.

Corinna, to whom Ovid addresses most of the *Amores,* seems to be a composite portrait of various real and imaginary mistresses. She appears now as a married woman,[82] now apparently as a maiden,[83] and again as a professional prostitute.[84] She has no distinct personality. She lacks entirely the reality of Delia and Cynthia. Ovid's attitudes toward love are as inconsistent as his references to his mistress. At one time he declares that he is no flit-about in love, but will remain ever constant.

Non mihi mille placent, non sum desultor amoris:
tu mihi, siqua fides, cura perennis eris.[85]

Soon, however, he recounts an intrigue with his mistress' waiting maid.[86] In another elegy he describes his infatuation for two girls

---

[79]Pro. I, VIII a, ll. 42 *et seq.*

[80]The *Amores* was first published in five books, later in three. During the time between the two editions, the *Heroides* was published. Duff, p. 586.

[81]Carter, *op. cit.,* Introduction p. XII.

[82]Ovid, *Amores* I, IV.

[83]*Amores* I, III.

[84]*Ibid.,* I, VIII.

[85]*Ibid.,* I, III, ll. 15-16.

[86]*Ibid.,* II, VII and VIII.

at once.[87]   Now he complains that his mistress is too closely guard-
ed;[88] now that his affair with her has lost its savor because access
to her is too easy.[89]   Again, in one of his most famous poems, he
declares that he cannot resist any temptation to love.

> Auferor ut rapida concita puppis aqua.
> Non est certa meos quae forma invitet amores—
> centum sunt causae cur ego semper amem.[90]

Ovid writes of love for love's sake.   He portrays loving as a
fine art, and is proud of his skill in its technique.   The lady does
not matter.   She merely affords him a chance to show his profi-
ciency as a lover.   He writes convincingly of physical passion; in
flattery and gallantry he is adept; but the tenderness of Catullus
and Tibullus and the passionate devotion of Propertius are alike
strange to his verse.   His tone is light, often to the point of flip-
pancy.   He is Alexandrian in license; and, at times, in his love of
mythological parallels, he is strongly touched with Alexandrian
learning.   In the form of his work he is the most flawless of the
Elegists.   His verse is smooth, graceful, apparently spontaneous.
There is no strain, no break in the easy flow of metre or sense.   His
art is perfectly concealed by its own perfection.

Certain traits of each of the Elegists are echoed in England in
the seventeenth century.   The whole love lyric convention of the
Cavalier poets, tho probably based directly on the Renaissance
courtly love conventions, is strongly influenced by the erotic tradition of the Augustans.   The ecstasy and disillusionment of Catullus, the passion and bitterness of Propertius, more rarely the wist-
ful or querulous tenderness of Tibullus sound recurringly thru
Caroline verse; and, dominating all, setting the tone of seventeenth
century erotic verse, swells the ever present motif of Ovid's sensuous and cynical love.

---

[87]*Ibid.*, II, x.
[88]*Ibid.*, II, II and III.
[89]*Ibid.*, II, XIX.
[90]*Ibid.*, II, IV, ll. 8-11.

CHAPTER II

ELEGIAC INFLUENCES ON THE "THREE SCHOOLS"

Though no investigation of the popularity of the Latin elegists in the sixteenth century has been made, it is evident from the number of editions printed before 1600 that their works, particularly those of Ovid, were somewhat widely read.[1] Elegiac influences are clearly visible thruout the first half of the seventeenth century, and reach their culmination in the poetry of Robert Herrick. They carry on a Latin erotic tradition which, though sometimes obscured, had never since the time of Chaucer been entirely submerged—a tradition which, mingled at times all but inextricably with the conventions of courtly and Platonic love, flows like an underground watercourse thru the work of the Cavalier lyrists, and frequently rises in springs of greater or less volume to the surface of their verse. It appears in varying degrees in the work of all three schools of the early seventeenth century. In the school of Spenser it is present, but for the most part subordinate to courtly or to pseudo-Platonic love; in the verse of Donne's followers it forces its way to the surface, contrary to the avowed tenets of the group; in the school of Jonson it flows openly on the surface, but is slender in volume until it rises like a fountain in the poetry of Herrick. As an introduction to the study of the elegiac influences in Herrick's verse, it seems advisable to make a cursory survey of such influences in the works of the more important of his early and immediate contemporaries. This survey is limited to direct borrowings from the Elegists, and does not attempt to deal with such indirect Latin trends as Marinism, which unquestionably was spreading from Italy to England.[2]

The first, chronologically, of the seventeenth century literary schools was that of Spenser. Among the Spenserians, Michael Drayton and Samuel Daniel each wrote one or more series of plain-

---

[1]Watts' *Bibliographica Brittanica* lists six editions of Propertius, four of Tibullus, and twenty of Ovid prior to 1600. Ovid alone had been translated at this time, and the only complete translation of his works (by Christopher Marlowe in or before 1598) was burned at Stationers' Hall by order of the Bishop of London and the Archbishop of Canterbury.

[2]Praz, Mario, *Secentismo e Marinismo in Inghilterra.*

tive love sonnets; and although, strictly speaking, these sonnets fall within the last decade of the sixteenth century, yet, since Daniel and Drayton are the most representative love lyrists of the school of Spenser, their work has been included in this study. Both these poets wrote in the conventions of courtly and Platonic love, rather than in the Latin erotic strain; but in their poetry some traces of elegiac influence may be found. Drayton, for instance, begins his *Idea's Mirror* as follows:

> Read here, sweet maid, the story of my woe,
> My life's complaint in *doleful elegies.*

In a sonnet to Idea he addresses Love:

> Thou purblind boy, since thou hast been so slack
> To wound her heart whose eyes have wounded me,
> Thus to my aid I lastly conjure thee.[3]

This last passage at once suggests Ovid's reproachful apostrophe to the same god:

> O numquam pro me satis indignate Cupido,
> O in corde meo desidiose puer.[4]

In the lines *To his Rival* Drayton writes:

> Therefore boast not
> Your happy lot,
> Be silent now you have her;
> The time I knew
> She slighted you
> When I was in her favor.
>
> But I'll not mourn
> But stay my turn,
> The wind may come about, Sir,
> And once again
> May bring me in
> And help to bear you out, Sir.

This is quite in the tradition of the Elegists. Tibullus in a similar situation wrote

---

[3]Drayton, *Idea,* Sonnet 36.
[4]Ovid, *Amores* II, ix, ll. 1-3.

at tu, qui potior nunc es, mea fata[5] timeto :
versatur celeri Fors levis orbe rotae.
non frustra quidam iam nunc in limine perstat
sedulus ac crebro prospicit ac refugit....

nescio quid furtivus amor parat. utere, quaeso,
dum licet: in liquida nam tibi linter aqua.[6]

Compare also Propertius' lines :

tu quoque, qui pleno fastus assumis amore,
credule, nulla diu femina pondus habet....

mendaces ludunt flatus in amore secundi.[7]

The closing lines of the sixty-first sonnet of the *Idea* sequence introduce another characteristic elegiac turn :

Now at the last gasp of Love's latest breath,
When, his pulse failing, Passion speechless lies....

Now if thou would'st, when all have given him over,
From death to life thou might'st him yet recover.

In a similar strain Propertius wrote :

....nunc est discedere tempus :
si dolor afuerit, crede, redibit amor.
non ita Carpathiae variant Aquilonibus undae....

quam facile irati verbo mutantur amantes.[8]

Drayton, like Propertius, declares that the only fame he wishes for his verse is that it may please his mistress :

I pass not I how men affected be
Nor who commend or discommend my verse;
It pleases me if I my plaints reherse,
And in my lines if she my love may see.[9]

---

[5]An alternative reading for *fata* is *furta*, i.e., "my intrigues." If this is adopted, then *quidam* (as J. P. Postgate points out in *Catullus, Tibullus, and Pervigilium Veneris*) means "I", and Drayton's poem is seen to be an even closer parallel.

[6]Tib. I, v, ll. 69 *et seq.*

[7]Pro. II, xxv, ll. 21-23 and 27.

[8]Pro. II, v, ll. 9 *et seq.*

[9]Drayton, *Idea's Mirror,* Amour 28.

Propertius, similarly, writes:

> ....haec mea fama est,
> hinc cupio nomen carminis ire mei.
> me laudent doctae solum placuisse puellae.[10]

Both Drayton and Ovid profess to write only for lovers:

> I marvel not thou feel'st not my delight
> Which never felt my fiery touch of love.
> But thou....
> ....whose spirit Love in his fire refines,
> Come thou and read, admire, applaud my lines.[11]

Compare Ovid's lines:

> ....Procul hinc, procul este, severae!
> non estis teneris apta theatra modis.
> me legat in sponsi facie non frigida virgo,
> et rudis ignoto tactus amore puer.[12]

Several of Drayton's other poems contain elegiac conventions. One sonnet in the *Idea's Mirror* sequence,[13] in more than Alexandrian style, cites twenty-one geographical proper names: Nile, Aetna, Indus, Pindus, Pelion, Ossa, Caucase, Delian, Cynthus, Olympus, Arar, Gallus, Cydnus, Ganges, Ister, Tagus, Po, Hypasis, Parnassus, Helicon, and Simois. Of these, all but one, Hypasis, appear in the works of at least one of the major Elegists. Other poems of Drayton that show elegiac traces are: *The Shepherd's Sirena*,[14] *Ode to the New Year*,[15] *The Shepherd's Garland* (Eclogue VII),[16]

---

[10]Pro. I, vii, ll. 9-12.

[11]Drayton, *Idea,* Sonnet 46.

[12]Ovid, *Amores* II, i, ll. 3-7.

[13]*Idea's Mirror,* Amour 20.

[14]Compare the lines:
> "Tagus and Pactolus
> Are to the debtor," etc.,

with Pro. I, xiv, l. 11; III, xviii, l. 28; and with Ovid, *Amores* I, xv, l. 34.

[15]"That spray to fame so fertile,
> The lover-crowning mirtle," etc.

Cf. Tib. I, iii, ll. 65-67; Ovid, *Amores* I, ii, l. 23.

[16]"Love taught my Muse her perfect skill," etc.

Cf. Pro. III, i; III, iii, and Ovid, *Amores* II, i, l. 35 *ad finem*.

The Muses' Elysium,[17] *The Quest of Cynthia,*[18] and several sonnets of the *Idea* sequence.[19]

Samuel Daniel's *Sonnets to Delia,* tho probably deriving the name of their heroine from Tibullus' mistress, owe less to the elegies than does Drayton's work. The plaintive tone of the sequence, however, suggests the Latin erotic strain, and a few of the common elegiac themes, such as the *carpe diem*[20] and the immortality-thru-verse[21] motifs, appear in Daniel's work. Certain favorite phrases of the English poet also suggest the Elegists. The *heart of flint* conceit, which appears in the verse of all the Elegists,[22] occurs again and again in Daniel's verse.[23] Delia's eyes are likened to "two radiant stars that shine,"[24] and both Propertius and Ovid had sung of their mistress' eyes as *sidera nostra.*[25] Ovid in a single poem likened love to bonds,[26] to flames,[27] and to a wound.[28] Daniel, in an astonishing *tour de force,* three times in one sonnet masses these conceits in a single line:

> Yet do I love, adore, and praise the same
> *That holds, that burns, that wounds me in this sort;*
> *And list not seek to break, to quench, to heal*
> *The bond, the flame, the wound that fest'reth so;*
> By knife, by liquor, or by salve to deal:
> So much I please to perish in my woe.[29]

---

[17]"There in perpetual summer's shade
      Apollo's prophets sit," etc.
    Cf. Ovid, *Amores* III, ix, ll. 59 *et seq.*

[18]"....Here our sports shall be
    Such as the golden world first saw," etc.
    Cf. Tib. II, iii, ll. 69 *et seq.* and Pro. III, xiii, ll. 25 *et seq.*

[19]Sonnets two and forty-three embody the ubiquitous motif of immortality thru verse, and in some phrases suggest an elegiac scource.

[20]Note sonnets XXXVI and XXXVII. The phrase *carpe diem* appears in Horace (*Carmina* I, xi, l. 8), and the theme is common elsewhere in Augustan poetry.

[21]Note Sonnet XXXIX.

[22]See Pro. I, xvi, l. 29; Tib. I, i, l. 64; Ovid, *Amores* I, xi, l. 9.

[23]See sonnets XI, XIII, XVIII, XIX, XXVI, and XXXIV.

[24]See sonnet XXX.

[25]Pro. II, iii, l. 14; Ovid, *Amores* II, xvi, l. 44. See also *Amores* III, iii, l. 9.

[26]"et nova captiva vincula mente feram," Ovid, *Amores* I, ii, l. 30.

[27]"Cedimus, an subitum luctando accendimus ignem?" *ibid.,* l. 9.

[28]"Ipse ego, praeda recens, factum modo vulnus habebo;" *ibid.,* l. 29.

[29]Daniel, Sonnet XIV.

The last line contains the characteristic elegiac paradox of the enjoyment of love's pains. Compare with these:

> et faveo morbo cum iuvat ipse dolor;[30]

and

> solus amor morbi non amat artificem.[31]

A few of Daniel's sonnets are Propertian in their extravagant protestations of loyalty;[32] but whatever opinion one holds of the sincerity of the Augustan lover, the piled up conceits of the English poet rob his vows of all power of conviction. In general, such elegiac influences as appear in Daniel's verse probably reached the poet only thru some intermediary source such as the verse of Marini.

Occasional touches of elegiac influence may be noted in the verse of Phineas Fletcher. The *Piscatory Eclogues* supply the familiar conceit, already cited in Daniel's work, of love's hatred of a cure for its ills:

> ....love doth more detest
> The cure and curer than the sweet disease.[33]

In the same eclogue the passage on the witching power of love:

> No writhel'd witch with spells of pow'rful charms,
> Or hellish herbs digg'd in as hellish night
> Gives to thy heart these oft and fierce alarms,
> But love, too hateful love, with pleasing spite

suggests Tibullus' lines:

> num te carminibus, num te pallentibus herbis
> devovit tacito tempore noctis anus?[34]

Compare with these also:

> Non facit hoc verbis [i.e., by charms], facie tenerisque
> lacertis
> devovet et flavis nostra puella comis;[35]

---

[30]Tib. II, v, l. 110.
[31]Pro. II, I, l. 58.
[32]Sonnets XXIX and XXXVIII. Cf. Pro. II, xxiv a, l. 34.
[33]Eclogue VI.
[34]Tib. I, viii, ll. 17-19.
[35]Tib. I, v, ll. 43 and 44.

and

> forma nihil magicis utitur auxiliis.[36]

The verse:

> Light winds, light air—her love more light than either

finds parallels in both Ovid and Propertius.[37] In Eclogue VII the clause "myrtles love the shore" is probably based on Ovid's line:

> cingere *litorea* flaventia tempora *myrto*.[38]

The poems of Sir John Beaumont are full of elegiac commonplaces—flames, darts, cupids, laurel garlands, etc., but show very little definite, traceable influence. Their author, however, in a panegyric written after his death, is himself compared to Ovid:

> I write not elegies....
>   with desire to rank
> My slender Muse 'mongst those who on the bank
> Of Aganippe's stream can better sing;
> ....   thy happy strains
> Did like the living source of Naso's song
> Flow to the ear.[39]

Francis Beaumont's *Charm* obviously borrows from Ovid much more than the name of its heroine:

> Come, my sweet Corinna, come;
>   Laugh, and leave thy fate deploring;
> Sable midnight makes all dumb
>   But they jealous husband's snoring
> And with thy sweet perfumed kisses
>   Entertain a stranger:
> Love's delight and sweetest bliss is
>   Got with greatest danger.

---

[36]Tib. I, viii, 1. 24.

[37]Ovid, *Amores* II, xvi, 1. 45; II, x, 1. 48; Pro. II, ix, 11. 33 *et seq.*

[38]Ovid, *Amores* I, i, 1. 29.

For other traces of elegiac influence compare:

Eclogue III: "You sea-born maids," etc.,

with Pro. I, xvii, 11. 25 *et seq;*

Eclogue V: "Poor boy: the wounds," etc.

with Pro. II, iv, 1. 7 and Tib II, iii, 1. 14.

[39]Thomas Hawkins, *An Elegy Dedicated to the Memory of Sir John Beaumont.*

Compare with this:

> tu quoque ne timide custodes, Delia, falle.
>   audendum est: fortes adiuvat ipsa Venus....

> illa docet molli furtim derepere lecto,
>   illa pedem nullo ponere posse sono.[40]

and

> nitimur in vetitum semper cupimusque negata.[41]

Another example of elegiac influence on the same poet occurs in *A Masque of the Gentlemen of Gray's Inn and the Inner Temple:*

> Jove will but laugh if you forswear.

Compare:

> scilicet aeterno falsum iurare puellis
>   di quoque concedunt, formaque numen habet.[42]

Francis Beaumont, as well as Sir John, was called a second Ovid:

> The wanton Ovid, whose inticing rimes
> Have with attractive wonder forc'd attention,
> No more shall be admir'd at; for these times
> Produce a poet whose more rare invention
> Will tear the love-sick myrtle from his brows
> T'adorn his temple with deserved boughs.[43]

As might be expected, the verse of Donne and his followers, on the whole, shows fewer traces of elegiac influence. Contemporary opinion of Donne's poetic standards and of his effect on English poetry, as well as a pertinent commentary on the common poetic usages of the period, is cogently expressed in the following lines by Thomas Carew:[44]

---

[40]Tib. I, ii, ll. 15 *et seq.*

[41]Ovid, *Amores* III, iv, l. 17.

[42]*Amores* III, iv, ll. 11-13.

[43]*To the Author,* by J. F. [John Fletcher].

[44]The works of Carew will be discussed under the school of Jonson, to which, in spite of some influences of Donne, they seem more closely allied. In many cases authorities differ in regard to the schools to which various poets are attributed. The question of schools has no vital bearing on the present paper, and no solution of debated cases has been attempted. The writer has simply used whatever classification has seemed most reasonable and most convenient for the purposes of this thesis.

AN ELEGIE UPON THE DEATH OF DR. DONNE, DEAN OF PAUL'S

The Muses' garden, with pedantic weeds
O'erspread, was purg'd by thee, the lazy seeds
Of servile imitation thrown away,
And fresh invention planted....
            ....the subtle cheat
Of sly exchanges, and the juggling feat
Of two-edg'd words, or whatsoever wrong
By ours was done the Greek or Latin tongue
Thou hast redeem'd....
            ....drawn a line
Of masculine expression which, had good
Old Orpheus seen, or all the ancient brood
Our superstitious fools admire, and hold
Their lead more precious than thy burnisht gold,
Thou hadst been their exchequer, and no more
They in each others' dung had search'd for ore.
But thou art gone, and thy strict laws will be
Too hard for libertines in poetry;
They will recall the goodly exil'd train
Of gods and goddesses, which in thy just reign
Was banish't....
Till....those old idols be
Ador'd again with new apostasie.
And so, whilst I cast on thy funeral pile
Thy crown of bays, O let it crack awhile,
And spit disdain, till the devouring flashes
Suck all the moisture up, then turn to ashes....
Here lie two flamens, and both these the best:
Apollo's first, at last the true God's priest.

Oddly enough, in the last six lines the poet has borrowed heavily
from the very Latin traditions he has just condemned, and has even
referred to Donne, the literary iconoclast, as priest to one of the
"exil'd train of gods."

Donne, himself, holds rather consistently to the standards he
set for poetry, and only rare echoes of the Augustans appear in
his verse. *The Indifferent,* however, undoubtedly owes much to
Ovid.[45] In Donne's other poems only a few scattered phrases suggest the Elegists.[46]

---

[45]Cf. *Amores* II, IV.

[46]E.g., with the first stanza of Donne's *The Sun Rising,* compare Ovid,
Amores I, XIII. Note particularly the resemblance of "Late school-boys and
sour prentices" to "tu pueros somno fraudas tradisque magistris."

Some members of Donne's school, however, in spite of the precepts of their poetic Mentor, show decided traces of Latin erotic influence. Even Crashaw, tho more "metaphysical" than Donne himself, paraphrased Catullus' Carmen V. Suckling definitely imitates Ovid, and writes:

> Yield all my love, but be withal as coy
> As if thou knew'st not how to sport and toy;
> The fort resigned with ease, men cowards prove,
> And lazy grow. Let me besiege my love;
> Let me despair at least three times a day,
> And take repulses upon each essay.
> Contract they smiles if that they go too far,
> And let such frowns be such as threaten war.
> Rather want faith to save thee, than believe
> Too soon: for credit me, 'tis true
> Men most of all enjoy when least they do.[47]

Compare Ovid's lines:

> speremus pariter, pariter metuamus amantes,
>   et faciat voto rara repulsa locum.
> quo mihi fortunam, quae numquam fallere curet?
>   nil ego, quod nullo tempore laedet, amo!....
> siqua volet regnare diu, deludat amantem.[48]

The lines:

> Rather want faith to save thee than believe
> Too soon,

may well be an echo of:

> a nimium faciles aurem praebere puellae,
>   discite desertae non temere esse bonae.[49]

Suckling's lines on *Love Turned to Hatred* also suggest one of Propertius' elegies.[50]

Among the followers of Donne, Abraham Cowley shows the greatest influence of the Elegists. Cowley writes chiefly in the tradition of Ovid, whom he considers—as did most other writers

---

[47]Suckling, *Upon A.M.*
[48]Ovid, *Amores* II, xix, ll. 5-9 and 33.
[49]Pro. II, xxi, ll. 15-17.
[50]See Pro. II, v, ll. 9-12.

of his age—the standard and model of erotic poets. Tho he declares that on one occasion, when in a rage, he took

> And out at window threw
> Ovid and Horace, all the chiming crew.[51]

it is safe to affirm that if the poet was ever guilty of such *lèse majesté,* he soon restored his slighted favorites to their wonted state. In *The Request* he mentions Ovid again, declaring presumptuously that concerning love he can teach

> More than thy skillful Ovid e'er did know.

Whether or not Cowley really believed that he could outdo his Roman master, it is certain that he consciously imitated him. In *The Inconstant* he writes in distinctly Ovidian vein:

> I never yet could see that face
>   Which had no dart for me;
> From fifteen years to fifty's space
>   They all victorious be.
>
> If tall, the name of proper slays;
> If fair, she's pleasant as the light;
> If low, her prettiness does please;
> If black, what lover loves not night?
> If yellow-haired, I love lest it should be
> Th' excuse to others for not loving me.[52]

To his *Epigram on the Power of Love* he prefixes Ovid's line:

> nullis amor est medicabilis herbis.[53]

Elegiac influence, moreover, appears in the following lines from the same epigram:

> Had any remedy for love been known,
> The god of physic, sure, had cur'd his own.

This couplet suggests obvious parallels from both Tibullus[54] and

---

[51]Cowley, *Ode upon Occasion of a Copy of Verses of My Lord Broghell's.*
[52]Cf. Ovid, *Amores* II, v, ll. 33 *et seq.*
[53]From *Remedia Amoris.*
[54]Tib. II, iii, l. 14.

Propertius.[55]   *The Monopoly,* moreover, with its apostrophe:

> Vain God! who woman dost thyself adore!

suggests Ovid's lines:

> di quoque concedunt, formaque numen habet.[56]

and

> di quoque habent oculos, di quoque pectus habent;[57]

and definite poems by Ovid are the models for Cowley's *Vain Love*[58] and his *Waiting Maid.*[59]

The other Elegists also find echoes in Cowley's verse. The vision of the Muse in *The Complaint* is very much in the tradition of Tibullus' vision of Apollo.[60]   *The Given Love* is elegiac in theme and tone, and certain lines, such as

> A curse upon the man who taught
> Women that love was to be bought,

suggest definite passages in Tibullus.[61]   Propertius' influence is evident in the lines from *The Cure*:

> Come doctor! use thy roughest art,
>   Thou canst not cruel prove;
> Cut, burn, and torture every part
>   To heal me of my love;[62]

and Cowley's *Ode from Catullus* is a paraphrase of Carmen XLV.

In the school of Jonson the elegiac influence is particularly important, culminating in the verse of Herrick; but in Jonson himself elegiac traces are surprisingly few and slight. That Jonson was familiar with the Elegists cannot be questioned. He not only

---

[55]Pro. II, i, ll. 57-59.
[56]Ovid, *Amores* III, iii, l. 12.
[57]*Ibid.,* l. 42.
[58]Cf. Ovid, *Amores* I, ii.
[59]Cf. *Amores* II, vii.
[60]Cf. Tib. III, iv, ll. 23 *et seq.*
[61]Cf. Tib. I, iv, ll. 59-61 and II, iv, ll. 27-29.
[62]Pro. I, i, ll. 26-29.

mentions them, but definitely declares his intention of emulating
them in his praise of a mistress:

> Was Lesbia sung by learn'd Catullus,
> Or Delia's graces by Tibullus?
> Doth Cynthia, in Propertius' song,
> Shine more than she the stars among?
>
> ....
>
> Or hath Corinna, by the name
> Her Ovid gave her, dimmed the fame
> Of Caesar's daughter?
>
> ....
>
> And shall not I my Celia bring
> Where men may see whom I do sing?
> Though I, in working of my song,
> Come short of all his learned[63] throng,
> Yet sure my tunes will be the best,
> So much my subject drowns the rest.[64]

Jonson, moreover, terms most of his erotic poems elegies, and occasionally in the thought or diction of these lyrics, echoes of the
Elegists can be traced. For example, he describes his mistress'
cheeks and Venus' as baths of "milk and roses,"[65] a conceit employed by Propertius in describing Cynthia's complexion.[66] Jonson's *Ode to Himself* beginning:

> Where dost thou careless lie
> Buried in ease and sloth

suggests Catullus' hendecasyllabic fragment:

> Otium, Catulle, tibi molestumst, etc.[67]

In general, tho Jonson's verse abounds in the commonplaces of
Latin erotic verse—

> all Cupid's armory,
> His flames, his shafts, his quiver, and his bow,[68]

---

[63]*Learned* (*doctus*) is the Augustan stock epithet for the Elegists.
[64]Ben Jonson, *An Ode*.
[65]Jonson, *His Discourse with Cupid and An Elegy*.
[66]Cf. "utque rosae puro lacte natant folia," Pro. II, iii, 1. 12.
[67]Catullus, *Carmen* II a.
[68]Jonson, *A Sonnet to the Noble Lady, the Lady Mary Wroth*.

the definite influences of the Elegists are so few and so slight as to be almost negligible.

All the leading poets of "the tribe of Ben," however, show decided influence of the Elegists. The poetry of Waller, for example, abounds in passages that, both in content and diction, parallel lines from the Augustan elegies. Under the title *A Song,* Waller writes:

> Behold the brand of beauty tost!
> See how the motion does dilate the flame,

lines that at once suggest the verse in which Ovid speaks of love as a brandished torch:

> vidi ego iactatas mota face crescere flammas.[69]

In another of his songs, Waller apostrophises a vision of his mistress:

> Colors of this glorious kind
> Come not from any mortal place.[70]

Compare Propertius' tribute to Cynthia's charms:

> Non non humani partus sunt talia dona.[71]

In his lines *Of Divine Love,* Waller treats the common classical convention, the Golden Age:

> This Iron Age (so fraudulent and bold)
> Touch'd with this love, would be an Age of Gold:
> Not as they feigned, that oaks should honey drop,
> Or land neglected bear an unsown crop;
> Love would make all things easy, safe, and cheap.

The tradition of the Golden Age appears in all the Elegists. The closest elegiac parallel to these lines occurs in Tibullus' verse:

> ipsae mella dabant quercus,[72] etc.

---

[69]Ovid, *Amores* I, II, 1. 11.
[70]Waller, *A Song.*
[71]Pro. II, III, 1. 27.
[72]Tib. I, III, 1. 45.

The classical superstition of spells which could force the moon down from the heavens appears twice in Waller's verse:

> But what so hard which numbers cannot force?
> So stoops the moon and rivers change their course.[73]

and

> numbers does repeat
> Which call descending Cynthia from her seat.[74]

In his lines *To a Friend of the Different Success of their Loves* Waller writes:

> Thrice happy pair! of whom we cannot know
> Which first began to love, or loves most now....
> I with a different fate pursued in vain
> The haughty Caelia.

Compare Propertius' verses:

> vos remanete, quibus facili deus annuit aure,
> sitis et in tuto semper amore pares.[75]

In his apostrophe *To the Mutable Fair,* Waller advises Caelia to flout and deceive her lover:

> For still to be deluded so
> Is all the pleasure lovers know,—

This advice undoubtedly echoes Ovid's dictum:

> Siqua volet regnare diu, deludat amantem,[76]

Moreover, Waller's next couplet:

> Who, like good falconers, take delight
> Not in the quarry but the flight

---

[73]Waller, *The Apology of Sleep.*
[74]Waller, *The Countess of Carlisle.*
For elegiac references to the calling of the moon from heaven see: Tib. I, VIII, 1. 21 and Pro. IV, v, 1. 13. For the turning back of streams see: Tib. I, II, 1. 44 and Ovid, *Amores* I, VIII, 1. 6.
[75]Pro. I, I, ll. 31-32.
[76]Ovid, *Amores* II, XIX, 1. 33.

closely parallels Ovid's lines:

> venator sequitur fugientia; capta relinquit
> semper et inventis ulteriora petit.[77]

The address *To Mrs. Braughton, Servant to Sacharissa* was probably inspired by Ovid's petition to Nape.[78] A less definite elegiac influence appears in such poems as *To Phyllis, To a Lady in Retirement,* and the song *Go, Lovely Rose,* all of which embody the common elegiac theme of the passing of beauty and youth.

The poems of Richard Lovelace show but slight traces of the elegies.[79] The poet knew the Augustan elegists, and mentions all of them except Propertius. Speaking of the "eternal laurel," he writes:

> Caesar to Gallus trundled it, and he
> To Maro; Maro, Naso, unto thee.
> Naso to his Tibullus flung the wreath,
> He to Catullus thus did it bequeath.[80]

Of this list of poets, Lovelace for the most part imitates only Catullus, several of whose *Carmina* he paraphrased.[81] One couplet from *Love Inthroned*:

> He has left his apish jigs
> and whipping hearts like gigs

was probably suggested by Tibullus' lines:

> namque agor ut per plana citus sola verbere turben
> quem celer adsueta versat ab arte puer.[82]

and the familiar topic of the Golden Age is treated in *Love Made in the First Age.* On the whole, however, Lovelace shows much less

---

[77]Ovid, *Amores* II, ix, ll. 9-11.

[78]*Amores* I, xi.

[79]Lovelace is sometimes considered as belonging to the school of Donne, and the small amount of elegiac influence in his verse suggests the school of Donne rather than that of Jonson.

[80]Lovelace, *On Sanazar's Being Honored.*

[81]The Carmina paraphrased are numbers XIII, XLVIII, LXX, LXXII, LXXV, LXXXII, LXXXVI, and LXXXVII.

[82]Tib. I, v, ll. 3-5.

influence of the Elegists than does any other member of the school
of Jonson.

Quite different in this respect is Thomas Campion: he not only
echoes the classical elegies in his verse but even composed epigrams
imitating in English elegiac metre and wrote a book of Latin elegies. In *There is None O None but You,* Campion writes:

> Sweet, afford me then your sight
> That, surveying all your looks,
> Endless volumes I may write
> And fill the world with envied books.

With this compare Propertius' lines:

> seu quicquid fecit sive est quodcumque locuta
> maxima de nihilo nascitur historia;[83]

and Ovid:

> te mihi materiem felicem in carmina praebe,
> provenient causa carmina digna sua.[84]

In his *Song,* beginning:

> When thou must home to shades of underground
> And there arriv'd, a new admired guest,
> The beauteous spirits do ingirt thee round,
> White Iope, blithe Helen, and the rest,
> To hear the stories of thy finished love
> From that smooth tongue whose music hell can move....

Campion probably echoes Propertius:

> quod si forte tibi properarint fata quietem,
>   illa sepulturae fata beata tuae.
> Narrabis Semelae quo sit formosa periclo,
>   credit et illa, suo docta puella malo;
> et tibi Maeonias omnes heroidas inter
>   primus erit nulla non tribuente locus.[85]

---

[83]Pro. II, ɪ, ll. 15-17.

[84]Ovid, *Amores* I, ɪɪɪ, ll. 19-21.

[85]Pro. II, xxvɪɪɪ, ll. 25 *et seq.* This likeness is noted by Bullen in Vivian's
edition of Campion.

The song beginning: "Shall I come, sweet Love, to thee," embodies the Augustan convention of the lover's spending his nights outside his mistress' door, a topic treated by both Ovid and Propertius:[86]

> Let me not, for pity, more
> Tell the long hours at your door....
> Do not mock me in thy bed,
> While these cold nights freeze me dead,—

Campion's lyric the first lines of which are

> O Love, where are thy shafts, they quiver, and they bow?
> Shall my wounds only weep, and he ungaged go?
> Be just and strike him, too, that does contemn thee so,

is much in the tradition of Ovid.[87] In *Leave Prolonging thy Distress,* Campion declares, "I die alone through her despite"—a declaration common among the followers of the Petrarchan love convention, but apparent also in the classical elegies,[88] so that it is impossible to determine Campion's source. Besides influences of the major Elegists, traces of Catullus appear in Campion's verse, particularly in the song containing the lines:

> Silly Traitress, who shall now thy careless
> tresses place? etc.[89]

He has also written a well-known translation of *Carmen V.*

The last poet to be discussed in this chapter is Thomas Carew, whose works clearly reflect influences of the Elegists—particularly of Ovid and, to a somewhat lesser extent, of Propertius. The following lines from *Persuasions to Love* are little more than a paraphrase of a passage from Ovid:

> Did the thing for which I sue
> Only concern myself, not you:
> Were men so framed as they alone
> Reaped all the pleasure, women none,
> Then had you reason to be scant;

---

[86] See Ovid, *Amores* I, vi and Pro. I, xvi.
[87] Cf. *Amores* II, ix.
[88] See Pro. II, i, l. 78 and Tib. III, ii, ll. 29 and 38.
[89] Cat. VIII, ll. 16 *et seq.*

> But 'twere a madness not to grant
> That which affords, if you consent,
> To you, the giver, more content
> Than me the beggar.

These lines are based on the following passage:

> quae Venus ex aequo ventura est grata duobus,
>   altera cur illam vendit et alter emit?
> cur mihi sit damno, tibi sit lucrosa voluptas,
>   quem socio motu femina virque ferunt?[90]

Carew's lines on *Ungrateful Beauty Threatened* are also modelled upon an elegiac original,—this time a passage from Propertius:

> Now, Celia, (since thou art so proud)
> 'Twas I that gave thee thy renown,
> Thou had'st in the forgotten crowd
> Of common beauties liv'd unknown,
> Had not my verse extoll'd thy name.

This is clearly imitated from:

> Falsa est ista tuae, mulier, fiducia formae,
>   olim oculis nimium facta superba meis.
> noster amor tales tribuit tibi, Cynthia, laudes.[91]

The first of Propertius' indignant farewells to Cynthia, with its figure of a ship leaving a treacherous haven to seek a safer one, evidently inspired the following lines from Carew's address *To his Unconstant Mistress:*

> Thus launch I off with triumph from thy shore
> To which my last fare-well: for never more
> Will I touch there to put to sea again,
> Blown with the churlish wind of thy disdain;
> Nor will I stop the course till I have found
> A coast that yields safe harbor and firm ground....
> Nor doubt I that for one that proves like you
> I shall find ten as fair and yet more true.

With this compare Propertius' lines:

---

[90]*Amores* I, x, ll. 33-37.
[91]Pro. III, xxiv, ll. 1-3.

dabis mihi, perfida, poenas;
et nobis aliquo, Cynthia, ventus erit.
inveniam tamen e multis fallacibus unam,
quae fieri nostro carmine nota velit,
nec mihi tam duris insultet moribus et te
vellicet: heu sero flebis amata diu.[92]

The same elegiac passage probably suggested also Carew's lines *To My Inconstant Mistress*. Addressing his verses *To his Mistress Retiring in Affection,* the poet writes:

But if my constant love shall fail to move thee,
Then know my reason hates thee, though I love thee.

In similar vein Ovid had written:

hac amor hac odium, sed, puto, vincit amor,
odero, si potero; si non, invitus amabo.[93]

Ovid's famous confession of susceptibility,[94] so popular with the seventeenth century poets, inspires two of Carew's shorter lyrics, *The Tinder* and *The Spark*. Catullus' ubiquitous Carmen V is translated in the well known *Song* beginning:

Come, my Celia, let us prove
While we may, the sports of love,

and *Persuasions to Joy* and *Persuasions to Love* also echo the perennially popular *carpe diem* theme. The Golden Age convention, occurring repeatedly in the elegies of Propertius and Tibullus, also appears in Carew's verse, most notably in his lines on *Love's Force*. On the whole, Carew seems to have been second only to Herrick in the amount of elegiac influence on his verse.

The brief survey attempted in this chapter indicates that a current of elegiac influence undoubtedly existed in the 17th century, hence that its notable outpouring in the verse of Herrick represented no isolated phenomenon but only a higher wave than usual of a ground swell common to much of the erotic poetry of the age. The parallels noted illustrate, among others, the following

[92]Pro. II, v, ll. 3-9.
[93]*Amores* III, xi, b. ll. 2-4.
[94]*Amores* II, iv.

characteristic elegiac motives: the *carpe diem* theme, the Golden Age, the fickleness of love and of fortune, love as a disease or as a wound, the swift passing of youth and love, the perjuries of love and the lenience of the gods toward broken vows, the vengeance of Cupid, susceptibility to many loves, and death caused by thwarted passion. The single elegy having the greatest influence is Ovid's famous declaration of susceptibility, *Amores* II, iv.

This discussion of the influence of the Latin erotic elegists on the verse of Herrick's contemporaries is avowedly an inadequate treatment of the subject. Minor poets, particularly those only slightly affected by the Elegists, have been omitted; and, in the case of the poets treated, only the most obvious parallels have been noted. The chapter is intended only as a background for and introduction to the following chapters, which attempt an intensive study of the Latin elegiac influences on the verse of Robert Herrick.

CHAPTER III

ELEGIAC THEMES—HERRICK'S VERSE

Of all the English poets of the seventeenth century, Herrick is by far the most thoroly saturated with the tradition of the minor Latin poetry of the reign of Augustus. So deeply is he steeped in the Roman literary conventions of the first century before Christ that he seems to employ them more naturally than he does the native poetic commonplaces of his own country and age. He is not satisfied to garnish his verse with classical similes or allusions. He is no mere borrower of neat Ovidian cynicisms or of passionate Catullan expostulations. He seldom directly translates even a single line of Latin verse. He is too practised a master of Roman *vers de société* to be content merely to adopt. He prefers to adapt, to echo, to vary, at times even to parody. The very scope and amount of the classical influences that worked upon him make it difficult to catch and classify them. There is in his verse so much of the Roman that it becomes elusive. In analyzing a compound it is often easier to locate a minute amount of an element than to dehydrate the mass. Herrick's poetry with all that is Latin removed would be rather thoroly dehydrated.

To be somewhat more specific as to Herrick's gleanings from the Augustans: he writes on their subjects; he adopts their themes; he echoes their moods; he adopts (as a literary convention, at least) their standards of values, both material and ethical; he is influenced strongly by their diction and, to a lesser extent, even by their tricks of verse structure. His mistresses have Romanized names. He invokes the Roman gods[1] in properly constructed Roman prayers

---

[1] Herrick addresses most of the gods of the Roman pantheon.
Note the following poems addressed to major or minor deities:

A Short Hymn to Lar	*To His Closet-Gods*
Another to Neptune	*To His Muse*
To Lar	*A Vow to Mars*
Lar's Portion and the Poet's Part	*A Vow to Minerva*
Departure of the Good Demon	*A Hymn to Cupid*
Short Hymn to Venus	*A Hymn to the Muses*
A Hymn to Juno	*A Request to the Graces*
Canticle to Bacchus	*To His Household Gods*

consisting of *prex* plus *votum*. Tho he is an Anglican clergyman, he repeatedly describes Christian ritual in terms of Roman sacrifices, very much as some of his predecessors of the Italian Renaissance might write of God the Father as Juppiter Optimus Maximus. In short, he takes over bodily the whole mass of Roman conventions and traditions that form the commonplaces of Augustan nonepic poetry; and he does this with such ease and lightness that in him the artificiality seems natural. In so doing, however, he sacrifices vigor and conviction to the museling of Augustan literary convention. No one is deeply stirred by his love or saddened by his griefs. The faint but pervasive wash of Roman local color gives to his poems an atmosphere of anachronism—hence, of unreality. It is only in his best poems on country life and customs that his sincerity sweeps him away from his classical moorings, and his verse catches the vigor and freshness of the English rural scenes he is describing. It is then, ironically enough, that he comes closest to his chief Augustan model, Tibullus.

Some of the conventional material that Herrick echoes is common to the elegists, to Horace, and to the *Georgics* or *Bucolics* of Virgil. From which source he drew it Herrick himself, perhaps, could not have told. The lighter poetry of the Augustan age was highly conventionalized. The poets of the period borrowed not only from earlier common sources, but from one another. Herrick's work is comparatively unstudied. The poet did not trouble to imitate a definite classical source. He merely wrote with a Roman atmosphere. Frequently this process resulted in an echo or variation of a definite and traceable Latin motif or of a common elegiac theme. At other times, the result was an indeterminate blending of Latin influences into a line that has a faint flavor of several classical lines but is not definitely related to any. It is difficult—not to say impossible—to determine from which of several conterminous springs a given cup of water is drawn. Hence some of the "echoes" quoted in this chapter may have had other originals besides the suggested passage from an elegist, or possibly may even have been based entirely on a parallel line from Horace or Virgil.

That Herrick's verse abounds in classical echoes cannot be questioned. That the influence of the elegists is the strongest classical element in his work is equally certain. In his well-known

poem *To Live Merrily and to Trust to Good Verses* Herrick lists
the major deities of his poetic Pantheon. The work is pertinent
enough to be quoted almost entire.

To Live Merrily and to Trust to Good Verses

Now is the time for mirth
    Nor cheek or tongue be dumb;
For with the flow'ry earth,
    The golden pomp is come.
     . . . . . .
Homer, this health to thee,
    In sack of such a kind
That it would make thee see,
    Though thou wert ne'er so blind.

Next Virgil I'll call forth
    To pledge this second health
In wine whose each cup's worth
    An Indian commonwealth.

A goblet next I'll drink
    To Ovid; and suppose
Made he the pledge, he'd think
    The world had all one nose.

Then this immensive cup
    Of aromatic wine,
Catullus, I quaff up
    To that terse muse of thine.

Wild I am now with heat,
    O Bacchus! cool thy rays,
Or frantic I shall eat
    Thy thyrse, and bite the bays.

Round, round, the roof does run
    And being ravish'd thus
Come, I will drink a tun
    To my Propertius.

Now, to Tibullus next
    This flood I drink to thee;
But stay, I see a text
    That this presents to me.

Behold! Tibullus lies
    Here burnt, whose small return
Of ashes scarce suffice
    To fill a little urn.

Trust to good verses then;
    They only will aspire,
When pyramids, as men,
    Are lost i' th' funeral fire.

And when all bodies meet
    In Lethe to be drown'd,
Then only numbers sweet
    With endless life are crown'd.[2]

Aside from the naming of the Elegists, the poem furnishes evidence that Herrick was familiar with them. The lines on Ovid:

"Made he the pledge, he'd think
    The world had all one nose"

not only play upon Ovid's name, "Naso," but probably echo Catullus' lines:

quod tu cum olfacies, deos rogabis
totum ut te faciant, Fabulle, nasum.[3]

Moreover, in the last two stanzas Herrick introduces a favorite theme common to Horace and the Elegists—a theme that he might have derived also from Chaucer or from a multitude of his own Renaissance contemporaries, but for the fact that his phrasing seems closest to classical prototypes: the eternity of fame thru verse.

---

[2]Edward Everett Hale, Jr., comments in his *Selections from the Poetry of Robert Herrick,* p. 166: "The climax is noteworthy; as genius wanes, he needs more wine; a health to Homer, a cup to Virgil, a goblet to Ovid, an 'immensive cup' to Catullus, a tun to Propertius, and a flood to Tibullus." But may the climax not be "noteworthy" for another reason? Does not Herrick list the poets in climactic order according to his personal feeling for them? Certainly, if one may judge from Herrick's verse, he read Tibullus more frequently than Homer. Note that it is Tibullus whose name is used to illustrate the eternity of fame.

[3]Catullus, *Carmen XIII,* ll. 13-14.

This theme appears recurringly in Herrick's work. It is difficult to trace his references to definite classical sources because so many of the Augustans celebrated immortality thru verse. All the Elegists embodied the idea,[4] and Horace expressed it supremely in his famous

> Exegi monumentum aere perennius,[5]

but it is noteworthy that the 1648 edition of the *Hesperides* has as its motto not Horace's better known line but a verse from Ovid:

> Effugient avidos Carmina nostra Rogos.[6]

Among Herrick's treatments of the idea note:

HIS POETRY HIS PILLAR[7]

> Behold this living stone
> I rear for me
> Ne'er to be thrown
> Down, envious Time, by thee.
>
> Pillars let some set up
> If so they please,
> Here is my hope,
> And my Pyramides.

With this compare:

> nam neque Pyramidum sumptus ad sidera ducti....

> mortis ob extrema condicione vacant.
> Aut illis flamma aut imber subducet honores
> annorum aut ictus pondere victa ruent,
> at non ingenio quaesitum nomen ab aevo
> excidet; ingenio stat sine morte decus.[8]

---

[4]See: Tib. I, IV, ll. 61 *et seq.;*
  Ovid, *Amores* I, III, ll. 25-26; I, XV, ll. 7 *et seq.;* II, IX, ll. 28-32;
  Pro. II, XXXIV, ll. 85 *et seq.;* III, I; III, II.
[5]Horace, *Lib. III, Carmen* XXX.
[6]Ovid, *Amores* III, IX, 1. 28.
[7]Herrick habitually renders the *monumentum* of the Augustans by *pillar.* Cf. his *The Pillar of Fame,* etc.
[8]Pro. III, II, ll. 19 and 22-26.

Herrick's lines *On Himself* deal with the same theme.

> Some parts may perish, die thou canst not all;
> The most of thee shall scape the funeral.

This may echo any or all of the following:

> Non omnis moriar, multaque pars mei
> vitabit Libitinam;[9]

> ergo etiam cum me supremus adederit ignis
> vivam, parsque mei multa superstes erit.[10]

> defugiunt avidos carmina sola rogos;[11]

Again, Herrick writes under the title *Upon Himself:*

> Thou shalt not all die; for while Love's fire shines
> Upon his altar, men shall read thy lines;
> And learn'd musicians shall to honor Herrick's
> Fame, and his name, both set and sing his lyrics.

This appears to be influenced by Horace's "non omnis moriar" and by Ovid's

> donec erunt ignes arcusque Cupidinis arma
> discentur numeri, culte Tibulle, tui.[12]

A variation on the theme appears in *The Mount of the Muses.*

> After thy labor take thine ease
> Here with the sweet Pierides.
> But if so be that men will not
> Give thee the laurel crown for lot,
> Be yet assur'd thou shalt have one
> Not subject to corruption.

With this compare:

> mollia, Pegasides, date vestro serta poetae....

---

9 Horace, *Carmina,* Lib. III, xxx, ll. 6-7.
10 Ovid, *Amores* I, xv, ll. 41-42.
11 *Ibid.,* III, ix, l. 28.
12 *Ibid.,* I, xv, ll. 27-28.

> at mihi quod vivo detraxerit invida turba,
> post obitum duplici faenore reddet Honos.[13]

The title *Mount of the Muses,* it will be noticed, is a translation of Propertius' phrase *Monte Sororum.*[14]

Somewhat the same idea is expressed by Ovid's lines:

> pascitur in vivis Livor; post fata quiescit,
> cum suus ex merito quemquqe tuetur honos.[15]

A less dignified treatment of the thought occurs in another *On Himself.* In this Herrick juxtaposes quite incongruous classical and Christian elements. One is tempted to classify the stanza as a burlesque, but it is probably only one of the all too common examples of the bad taste of which Herrick was capable.

ON HIMSELF

> The work is done; young men and maidens set
> Upon my curls the myrtle coronet,
> Wash'd with sweet ointments, thus at last I come
> To suffer in the Muses' martyrdom,
> But with this comfort, if my blood be shed,
> The Muses will wear black when I am dead.

This free working of the classical convention may have been suggested by either of the two Latin passages just quoted. The reference to the *myrtle* coronet especially suggests Ovid's

> sustineamque coma metuentem frigora myrtum.[16]

As a final illustration of Herrick's treatment of eternal fame won by verse, note his *Pillar of Fame,* a poem written in the shape of the object described.

THE PILLAR OF FAME

> Fame's pillar here at last we set,
> Out-during marble, brass, or jet;
> Charm'd and enchanted so

---

[13]Pro. III, i, ll. 19 and 21-22.
[14]*Ibid.,* l. 17.
[15]Ovid, *Amores* I, xv, ll. 39-40.
[16]Ovid, *Amores* I, xv, l. 37.

> As to withstand the blow
> Of   o v e r t h r o w
> Nor shall the seas
> O r   o u t r a g e s
> Of Storms o'erbear
> What   we   uprear;
> Tho kingdoms fall,
> This pillar never shall
> Decline or waste at all;
> But stand forever by his own
> Firm and well-fix'd foundation.
> To his book's end this last line he'd have plac'd:
> Jocund his Muse was, but his life was chaste.

This again echoes a combination of Horace[17] and the Elegists. Compare with it:

> Ergo, cum silices, cum dens patientis aratri
>   depereant aevo, carmina morte carent.
> Cedant carminibus reges regumque triumphi.[18]

The last two lines imitate:

> Nam castum esse decet pium poetam
> ipsum, versiculos nihil necessest,[19]

lines which Herrick also followed in his epigram *Poets:*

> Wantons we are; and though our words be much,
> Our lives do differ from our lines by much.

Both Herrick and the Elegists promise immortality to those whom they celebrate in their verse, and both address such promises either to their mistresses or to their patrons; but there is little likeness in their respective methods of treating the theme. The Latin poets are comparatively simple and dignified; Herrick, doubtless under the influence of the Marinism of contemporary Italy, is figurative and conceited.

Another common theme of Horace and the Elegists that is reworked again and again in Herrick's verse is the swift passing

---

[17]Horace, *Carmina*, Lib. III, xxx.
[18]Ovid, *Amores* I, xv, ll. 31 *et seq.*
[19]Catullus, *Carmen* XVI, ll. 5-6.

of youth and love—the *carpe diem* motif. Catullus uses it in his famous *Carmen V*,[20] perhaps the best known of his poems. Both Tibullus and Propertius revert to the theme,[21] now wistfully, now with zeal or feigned bravado. Herrick treats the idea repeatedly, sometimes simply, with a touch of the true classical spirit; oftener lightly, almost mockingly; again, in conventional, conceited verse. Herrick at his best could sometimes assimilate a classical thought, and re-express it with all the freshness of originality in fluid, spirited English verse. He did this with remarkable *verve* and charm in his well known lines *To the Virgins*.

To the Virgins To Make Much of Time

Gather ye rosebuds while ye may,
    Old Time is still a-flying;
And this same flower that smiles to-day,
    To-morrow will be dying.

The glorious lamp of heaven, the sun,
    The higher he's a-getting,
The sooner will his race be run,
    And nearer he's to setting.

That age is best which is the first,
    When youth and blood are warmer;
But being spent, the worse and worst
    Times still succeed the former.

Then be not coy, but use your time
    And while ye may, go marry;
For having lost but once your prime,
    You may for ever tarry.

So far as the thought is concerned, each stanza may well be an echo of a passage from one of the Elegists. With stanza one compare:

---

[20]"Soles occidere et redire possunt:
nobis cum semel occidit brevis lux,
nox est perpetua una dormienda."
            Catullus, *Carmen* V, ll. 4-6.
[21]See Tib. I, i, ll. 70 *et seq.;* I, iv, ll. 28 *et seq.;* I, viii, ll. 41 *et seq.;* and Pro. I, xix, ll. 25-26; II, xv, ll. 23-24 and 49 *et seq.;* III, xxv.

> .... transiit aetas
> quam cito! non segnis stat remeatve dies.
> quam cito purpureos deperdit terra colores,
> quam cito formosas populus alta comas.[22]

The second stanza might be considered a variation of

> Nox tibi longa venit, nec reditura dies.[23]

Stanza three inverts a passage from Tibullus:

> Iam subrepet iners aetas, nec amare decebit,
> dicere nec cano blanditias capite.
> nunc levis est tractanda Venus, dum frangere postes
> non pudet et rixas inseruisse iuvat.[21]

The last stanza echoes:

> at te poena manet, ni desinis esse superba.
> quam cupies votis hunc revocare diem![25]

or

> at si tardus eris, errabis. Transiit aetas
> quam cito![26]

In this poem Herrick's genius has fused his classical elements into an artistic whole which, on the surface, does not even suggest Latin influence, but nevertheless embodies classical ideas in a form, simple, graceful, and appropriate. In some of his treatments of the theme, however, Herrick is less fortunate. Too often he crowds his verse with affected and conventional parallels, with such Corinthian elaborations as the Renaissance loved to make of classical prototypes. Note for example the following:

A MEDITATION FOR HIS MISTRESS

> You are a tulip seen to-day,
> But, dearest, of so short a stay,
> That where you grew, scarce man can say.

---

[22]Tib. I, IV, ll. 27-30.
[23]Pro. II, XV, l. 24.
[21]Tib. I, I, ll. 71-74.
[25]Tib. I, VIII, ll. 77-78.
[26]Tib. I, IV, ll. 27-28.

> You are a lovely July-flower,
> Yet one rude wind or ruffling shower,
> Will force you hence, and in an hour.
>
> You are a sparkling rose i' th' bud,
> Yet lost ere that chaste flesh and blood
> Can show where you or grew or stood.
>
> You are a full-spread, fair-set vine,
> And can with tendrils love entwine,
> Yet dried, ere you distil your wine.
>
> You are like balm, inclosed well
> In amber, or some crystal shell,
> Yet lost ere you transfuse your smell.
>
> You are a dainty violet,
> Yet wither'd, ere you can be set
> Within the virgin's coronet.
>
> You are the queen all flowers among,
> But die you must, fair maid, ere long,
> As he, the maker of this song.

This prolix effusion has been quoted in full to give one example of the lengths to which, even in a reworking of a classical theme, Herrick's fancy and his tendency toward conceits could lead him. The one thought of the poem was expressed by Propertius thus:

> nec forma aeternum aut cuipiam est fortuna perennis:
> longius aut propius mors sua quemque manet;[27]

and by Tibullus:

> formae non ullam fata dedere moram.[28]

A shorter example of Herrick's tendency to overdo floral parallels is:

> The lily will not long endure,
> Nor the snow continue pure;
> The rose, the violet one day,
> See, both these lady-flowers decay;
> And you must fade as well as they.[29]

---

[27]Pro. II, xxviii a, ll. 57-58.
[28]Tib. I, iv, l. 36.
[29]Herrick, *The Cruel Maid.*

Other flower-poems on the same theme are *To a Bed of Tulips* and the well known *To Daffodils*. Again, the poet writes:

> No sound recalls the hours once fled
> Or roses being withered.
> . . . . . .
> Then live we mirthful, while we should,
> And turn the iron age to gold.
> Let's feast and frolic, sing and play,
> And thus less last than live our day.
> . . . . . .
> And that we'll do, as men who know,
> Some few sands spent,[30] we hence must go,
> Both to be blended in the urn
> From whence there's never a return.[31]

This poem, perhaps, owes more to Horace than to the Elegists, since it does not stress love. It suggests, however, Propertius' lines:

> tu modo, dum licet, o fructum ne desere vitae!
> . . . . . .
> ac veluti folia arentes liquere carollas,
>   quae passim calathis strata natare vides,
> sic nobis, qui nunc magnum speramus amantes,
>   forsitan includet crastina fata dies.[32]

Herrick is more characteristically elegiac in the tone of his

To Myrrha Hard-hearted

> Fold now thine arms, and hang the head
> Like to a lily withered:
> . . . . . .
> And all because, fair maid, thou art
> Insensible of all my smart,
> And of those evil days that be
> Now posting on to punish thee.

Compare:

---

[30]Note the ablative absolute construction brought over into English.

[31]Herrick, *A Paranoeticall or Advisive Verse to his Friend Mr. John Wicks.*

[32]Pro. II, xv, ll. 49 and 51 *et seq.*

> heu sero revocatur amor seroque iuventas
> cum vetus infecit cana senecta caput.
>
> . . . . . .
>
> at tu dum primi floret tibi temporis aetas
> utere: non tardo labitur illa pede.[33]

and

> at te poena manet, ni desinas esse superba
> quam cupies votis nunc revocare diem.[31]

Propertius in the same spirit writes:

> eventum formae disce timere tuae.[35]

Another group of poems on this theme, tho Horatian rather than elegiac in tone, suggests the Elegists in phraseology. Note *A Lyric to Mirth:*

> While the milder Fates consent,
> Let's enjoy our merriment:
> Drink and dance and pipe and play,
> Kiss our dollies night and day.
> Crown'd with clusters of the vine,
> Let us sit and quaff our wine,
> Sing o'er Horace; for ere long
> Death will come and mar the song.

Compare with the first line:

> interea, dum fata sinunt, iungamus amores[36]

and

> cum nos fata sinunt, oculos satiemus amore.[37]

With the last line of Herrick's stanza, compare:

> iam veniet tenebris mors adoperta caput.[38]

---

[33]Tib. I, VIII, ll. 41-42 and 47-48.
[31]*Ibid.*, ll. 77-78.
[35]Pro. III, xxv, l. 18.
[36]Tib. I, I, l. 69.
[37]Pro. II, xv, l. 23.
[38]Tib. I, I, l. 70.

and

longius aut propius mors sua quemque manet.[39]

Another stanza in the same tradition is

BEST TO BE MERRY

Fools are they who never know
How the times away do go.
But for us, who wisely see
Where the bounds of black death be,
Let's live merrily, and thus
Gratify the Genius.

Black (ater) as an attribute of death is used by both Horace and Tibullus. Other poems of the same type are *To Electra, To Sappho, An End Decreed, To Be Merry,* and *A Lyrick to Mirth.* Note also the first five stanzas of *His Age.*

Herrick wrote on the same theme several epigramatic couplets—among them the following:

TO YOUTH

Drink wine, and live here blitheful while ye may.
The morrow's life too late is, Live today.

TO LIVE FREELY

Let's live in haste, use pleasures while we may.
Could life return, 'twould never lose a day.

TO ENJOY THE TIME

While Fates permit us, let's be merry;
Pass all we must the fatal ferry.

In form these suggest the elegiac epigrams of Catullus. The thought again echoes some of the elegiac lines quoted above. With Herrick's advice to youth compare:

at tu dum primi floret tibi temporis aetas
utere: non tardo labitur illa pede.[40]

---

[39]Pro. II, xxviii a, 1. 58.
[40]Tib. I, viii, ll. 47-48.

With *To Live Freely* compare:

> at si tardus eris, errabis. Transiit aetas
> quam cito! non segnis stat remeatve dies.[41]

In the last quoted of Herrick's couplets, the clause "while Fates permit us" is an exact translation of Tibullus' "dum fata sinunt"[42] and of Propertius' "dum nos fata sinunt."[43] Note also the somewhat undignified reference to classical mythology in

> "Pass all we must the fatal ferry."

The last stanza of *Corinna's Going A-Maying* is one of Herrick's happiest treatments of the theme.

> Come let us go, while we are in our prime,
> And take the harmless folly of the time.
> We shall grow old apace and die
> Before we know our liberty.
> Our life is short, and our days run
> As fast away as does the sun,
> And as a vapor, or a drop of rain
> Once lost, can ne'er be found again,
> So when or you or I are made
> A fable, song, or fleeting shade
> All love, all liking, all delight
> Lies drown'd with us in endless night.
> Then while time seres, and we are but decaying,
> Come, my Corinna, let's go a-Maying.

A natural corollary to the brevity-of-life motif of the Elegists was a constant and often poignant awareness of the imminence of Death.

> iam veniet tenebris Mors adoperta caput.[44]

Coupled with this was a deep interest in the disposal of the body after death—an interest traditional and natural to a Roman because of the ancient belief that unless the body was properly buried,

---

[41] Tib. I, iv, ll. 27-28.
[42] Tib. I, i, l. 69.
[43] Pro. II, xv, l. 23.
[44] Tib. I, i, l. 70.

the soul could not rest. This whole tradition and the accompany-
ing interest in funeral rites[45] are taken over by Herrick. Following the example of the Elegists,[46] he writes to one or another of his
hypothetical mistresses explicit directions for his burial. If she
will but perform the due rites, he tells her,

> ergo cum tenuem fuero mutatus in umbram
>   candidaque ossa supra nigra favilla teget
> ante meum veniat longos incompta capillos
>   et fleat ante meum maesta Neaera rogum....
>
> praefatae ante meos manes animamque recentem
>   perfusaeque pias ante liquore manus,
> pars quae sola mei superabit corporis, ossa
>   incinctae nigra candida veste legent,
> et primum annoso spargent collecta lyaeo,
>   mox etiam niveo fundere lacte parent,
> post haec carbaseis umorem tollere velis
>   atque in marmorea ponere sicca domo.
> illic quas mittit dives Panchaia merces
>   Eoique Arabes, dives et Assyria,
> et nostri memores lacrimae fundantur eodem:
>   sic ego componi versus in ossa velim.
>   Tib. III, ii, ll. 9 *et seq.*

Then shall my ghost not walk about but keep
Still in the cool and silent shades of sleep.[47]

These lines occur in the following poems in which Herrick gives
the most detailed instructions as to his burial rites.

To Perilla

'Twill not be long, Perilla, after this,
That I must give thee the supremest kiss;
Dead when I am, first cast in salt, and bring

----

[45]As an example of specific directions for funeral rites, written by an
elegist to his mistress, note the following lines from an elegy ascribed to
"Lygdamus" (an unidentified elegist whose works are commonly included
in the third book of Tibullus).

[46]For references in the Elegists to funeral rites, see:

Tib. I, i, ll. 61 *et seq.;* I, iii, ll. 5 *et seq.;* III, ii, ll. 9 *et seq.;* Pro. I, xvii,
ll. 19 *et seq.;* II, xiii a, III, xvi, ll. 21 *et seq.;* IV, vii, ll. 25 *et seq.*

[47]Herrick, *To Perilla.*

> Part of the dream from that religious spring,
> With which, Perilla, wash my hands and feet;
> That done, then wind me in that very sheet
> Which wrapped thy smooth limbs when thou didst implore
> The God's protection but the night before.
> Follow me weeping to my turf and there
> Let fall a primrose, and with it a tear:
> Then lastly, let some weekly-strewings be
> Devoted to the memory of me.

In this poem the rites which Herrick requests to have performed do not follow closely their classical models. The poet has blended (as he not infrequently does) Pagan and Christian customs and added, besides, some touches suggested by his own imagination. Certain analogies with the Elegists may, however, be noted. Both Lygdamus and Herrick include the use of lustral water in their rites.[48] The shade of Cynthia, Propertius' mistress, asks why hyacinths were not cast upon her at her burial.[49] Herrick, too, asks for flowers—primroses, however, rather than hyacinths. Finally, Herrick's phrase "supremest kiss" is a literal translation of Propertius' "oscula suprema."[50]

A similar poem is

His Charge to Julia at his Death

> Dearest of thousands, now the time draws near,
> That with my lines, my life must full-stop here.[51]
> Cut off thy hairs, and let thy tears be shed
> Over my turf, when I am buried.
> Then for effusions, let none wanting be,
> Or other rites that do belong to me;
> As love shall help thee, when thou do'st go hence
> Unto everlasting residence.

The rites indicated in this stanza are somewhat more classical. Disheveling the hair and cutting off locks of it was a common practice of Roman women mourners, and the custom is repeatedly referred to by the Elegists. Note, for example, the lines:

---

[48]Tib. III, ii, l. 16.
[49]Pro. IV, vii, l. 33.
[50]Pro. II, xiii a, l. 29.
[51]Pro. I, xvi, l. 21.

> ante meum veniat longos incompta capillos
> et fleat ante meum maesta Neaera rogum.[52]

As to the "effusions" mentioned by Herrick, the word appears to refer to the offerings of wine or milk poured upon the ashes of a cremated body. Lygdamus speaks of the custom thus:

> pars quae sola mei superabit corporis, ossa
> incinctae nigra candida veste legent,
> et primum annoso spargent collecta lyaeo,
> mox etiam niveo fundere lacte parent.[53]

It seems doubtful, however, whether Herrick wishes his body to be burned. The "effusions" may refer simply to drink offerings poured out for his *Manes*. Herrick mentions this custom in the lines:

> .... I bring
> Unto thy ghost th' effused offering;[54]

and

> One night i' th' year, my dearest beauties, come
> And bring these dew-drink offerings to my tomb.[55]

In some of Herrick's other poems on funeral rites, the influence of the Elegists can be traced more definitely. In *His Embalming to Julia,* Herrick writes:

> Give thou my lips but their supremest kiss.

With this compare:

> osculaque in gelidis pones suprema labellis.[56]

In the poems quoted above, it has appeared that Herrick intended his body to be buried rather than burned after the custom of the ancients. In the following lines, however, he follows more closely the Roman tradition.

---

[52]Tib. III, ii, ll. 11-12.
[53]Tib. III, ii, ll. 17-20.
[54]Herrick, *To the Reverend Shade of his Religious Father.*
[55]Herrick, *To His Lovely Mistresses.*
[56]Pro. II, xiii a, l. 29.

To Anthea

If, dear Anthea, my hard fate it be
To live some few sad hours after thee,
Thy sacred corse with odors I will burn,
And with my laurel crown thy golden urn.
Then holding up there such religious things
As were (time past) thy holy filitings,
Near to thy reverend pitcher I will fall
Down dead for grief and end my woes withal.
So there in one small plot of ground shall lie
Anthea, Herrick, and his poetry.

Propertius, giving to Cynthia directions for his funeral, mentions the incense, the urn, and the laurel to which Herrick refers in the stanza above.

oscula in gelidis pones suprema labellis
    cum dabitur Syrio munere plenus onyx.
deinde, ubi suppositus cinerem me fecerit ardor,
    accipiat manes parvula testa meos,
et sit in exiguo laurus super addita busto.[57]

Propertius also refers to the same rites in:

afferet huc unguenta mihi sertisque sepulcrum
    ornabit;[58]

and in Cynthia's demand:

cur nardo flammae non oluere meae?[59]

The Roman poet desires that his books shall be buried with him.

sat mea sit magna, si tres sint pompa libelli
    quos ego Persephonae maxima dona feram.[60]

Similarly, Herrick in the poem quoted above declares that his poems shall lie in the grave with him and his mistress. In another

---

[57]Pro. II, xiii a, ll. 29-34.
[58]Pro. III, xvi, ll. 23-24.
[59]Pro. IV, vii, l. 32.
[60]Pro. II, xiii a, ll. 25-27.

short poem he mentions again funereal laurels.   This time they are
to be planted on his grave—as Propertius requests in his directions
to Cynthia.[61]

To LAURELS

A funeral stone
Or verse I covert none
But only crave
Of you that I may have
A sacred laurel springing from my grave.

In *The Cruel Maid,* Herrick refers again, but vaguely, to
funeral rites.

When you shall see that I am dead
For pity let a tear be shed;
And, with your mantle o'er me cast,
Give my cold lips a kiss at last.
. . . .
Next hollow out a tomb to cover
Me, the most despised lover,
And write thereon, "This, Reader, know;
Love kill'd this man!"   No more but so.

The fourth line of this stanza echoes yet again Propertius'

"Thou shalt press a last kiss upon my cold lips."[62]

The last couplet introduces a characteristic elegiac turn,—an
epitaph ascribing the lover's death to the cruelty of his mistress.
Compare with it:

sed tristem mortis demonstret littera causam
    atque haec in celebri carmina fronte notet:
Lygdamus hic situs est. Dolor huic et cura Neaerae,
    Coniugis ereptae, causa perire fuit.[63]

Note also:

Huic misero fatum dura puella fuit.[64]

---

[61]Pro. II, XIII a, 1. 33.
[62]Pro. II, XIII a, 1. 29.
[63]Tib. III, II, 11. 27 *et seq.*
[64]Pro. II, I, 1. 78.

Funereal customs are vaguely mentioned in several other poems of Herrick's: for example, in one of his poems addressed *To Perilla,* in *His Return to London,* and in one of his numerous pieces *To Julia.* His *To His Dying Brother, Master William Herrick* calls to mind Catullus' elegies on his dead brother, and the lines

> .... when we part,
> Then even then, I will bequeath my heart
> Into thy loving hands; for I'll keep none
> To warm my breast when thou, my pulse, art gone,

tho disfigured by a conceit, suggest Catullus'

> Tu mea tu moriens fregisti commoda, frater, ...
> omnia tecum una perierunt gaudia nostra,
>   quae tuus in vita dulcis alebat amor.[65]

In his *Ode to Master Endymion Porter upon his Brother's Death,* Herrick borrows a parallel from Catullus' famous Carmen V[66]—a lyric in hendecasyllables but in tone and theme much like the elegies.

Compare:

> Days may conclude in nights, and suns may rest,
>   As dead, within the west;
> Yet the next morn regild the fragrant east.
>
> Alas for me; that I have lost
>   E'en all almost.
> Sunk is my sight; set is my sun;
> And all the loom of life undone.

and

> soles occidere et redire possunt:
> nobis cum semel occidit brevis lux,
> nox est perpetua una dormienda.[67]

In spirit and tone, moreover, this is closest of all Herrick's poems to the beautiful elegiac lament of Catullus for his brother:

---

[65] Cat. LXVIII, ll. 21 and 23-24.
[66] Grosart, in his edition of Herrick, notes this influence.
[67] Cat. Car. V, ll. 4-6.

> .... ei misero frater adempte mihi,
> ei misero fratri iucundum lumen ademptum,
> tecum una totast nostra sepulta domus;
> omnia tecum una perierunt gaudia nostra,
> quae tuus in vita dulcis alebat amor.[68]

Herrick was familiar with all the Augustan elegists. His works show influences of them all. To one of the group, however, he is especially bound by a noteworthy community of interests. Four main themes—country life, rural religious festivals, praise of a patron, and love of a mistress—dominate the whole body of the works of Tibullus. Of these Herrick celebrates every one, and, like Tibullus, often fuses two or more of them. Note, for example, his lines on *The Country Life.* An analysis of the verses quoted below—approximately the first quarter of the poem—reveals the presence of several related and characteristically Tibullan motifs: country life, eulogy of a patron (here represented by the poet as leading an idyllic and idealized existence suggesting the Golden Age), and content with one's own lot. Elegiac parallels are placed in the adjoining column.

THE COUNTRY LIFE

(To the Honoured Mr. Endymion Porter, Groom of the Bedchamber to His Majesty)

Divitias alius fulvo sibi
  congerat auro
me mea paupertas vita traducat
  inerti.[69]

Sweet country life, to such unknown
Whose lives are others' not their
  own,
    ....

nec vagus ignotis repetens
  compendia terris
presserat externa navita merce
  ratem;[70]
(from a description of the
Golden Age)

Thou never plough'st the ocean's
  foam
To seek and bring rough pepper
  home;
    ....

---

[68]Cat. LXVIIIa, ll. 52-56.
[69]Tib. I, i, ll. 1 and 5.
[70]Tib. I, iii, ll. 39-40.

iam mihi iam possim contentus
    vivere parvo
nec semper longae deditus
    esse viae.[71]

Nor with the loss of thy lov'd rest,
Bring'st home the ingot from the
    West;
No, thy ambition's masterpiece
Flies no thought higher than a fleece;
    . . . .

parva seges satis est; satis
    est requiescere lecto
si licet et solito membra
    levare toro.[72]

But walk'st about thine own dear
    bounds,
Not envying others' larger grounds,
For well thou know'st, 'tis not
    th' extent
Of land makes life, but sweet
    content.

In the rest of the poem Herrick does not so nearly parallel the thought of Tibullus, but in tone and spirit he approaches him more closely. Tibullus is his inspiration rather than his model. Both the Devonshire poet and the Roman have a sincere love for the country. Each treats native and contemporary rural customs with a real feeling and picturesque charm. {Each of them describes at some length the country feasts and religious festivals of his own time.[73]} In many ways the agricultural life known to the Roman poet was not radically different from that of Herrick's time. Both poets speak of flocks that must be protected from wolves, of "wanton" herds and plodding oxen, of sowing and reaping, of growing grain, of orchards heavy with fruit, of shady trees, clear-flowing streams, flowers, birds—of all the idyllic aspects and trappings of nature that appeal so strongly to the city-dweller, whether of London or Rome.[74]

---

[71]Tib. I, i, ll. 25-26.

[72]Tib. I, i, ll. 43-44.

[73]E.g., see the following poems by Herrick: *The Hock-cart or Harvest Home, The Maypole, Corinna's Going A-Maying, The Wake, Ceremonies for Christmas, Christmas Eve, Another Ceremony, Ceremonies for Candlemas Eve, The Ceremonies for Candlemas Day, Ceremony upon Candlemas Eve, Saint Distaff's Day, Twelfth Night.*

For elegiac treatment of rural festivals, see: Tib, I, i, ll. 10 *et seq.;* I, x, ll. 15 *et seq.;* II, i; II, ii; II, v, ll. 79 *et seq;* Ovid III, x; III, xiii; Pro. II, xxxiv, ll. 70 *et seq.;* IV, vi.

[74]See: *A Country Life: To his Brother, Mr. Thomas Herrick, A New Year's Gift to Sir Simeon Steward, His Content in the Country, The Coun-*

The rural festivals, too, of the Italian peasants and of the Devonshire rustics have many a similar feature. Both Tibullus and Herrick describe harvest festivals and offerings of first fruits, observances of ancient rites to insure plentiful crops or to secure the flocks from beasts of prey, rustic dances and rustic love-making, feasts spread on the greensward, healths to masters or sweethearts, much eating and more drinking—whether of Chian and Falernian or wassail and "nut-brown mirth"—and, with it all, a homely but sincere devotion to the God or the gods of the harvest.

Herrick's *A Country Life: To his Brother,* tho perhaps more Horatian than elegiac, contains passages strongly reminiscent of the Elegists—particularly of Tibullus. Its theme:

> To teach man to confine desires
> and know that riches have their proper stint
> In the contented mind, not mint;

is elaborated by Tibullus as well as by Horace. Compare:

> iam mihi, iam possim contentus vivere parvo[75]

and

> .... ego composito securus acervo
> dites despiciam despiciamque famem.[76]

The English poet's idea of the *summum bonum* of country life corresponds closely with Tibullus'. Compare Herrick's lines:

> But that which makes most sweet thy country life
> Is the affection of a wife....
>
> By whose warm side thou dost securely sleep....
>
> With those deeds done by day which ne'er affright
> Thy silken slumbers in the night;[77]

with Tibullus':

---

try Life (to Endymion Porter).

    For rural descriptions by the Elegists see: Tib. I, i; I, ii, ll. 70 *et seq.;* I, v, ll. 21 *et seq.;* I, x, ll. 15 *et seq.;* Pro. II, xix.
    [75]Tib. I, i, l. 25
    [76]*Ibid.,* ll. 77-78.
    [77]Herrick, *A Country Life,* ll. 31 *et seq.*

> quam iuvat immites ventos audire cubantem
> et dominam tenero continuisse sinu;[78]

and the same poet's word to Delia:

> et te dum liceat teneris retinere lacertis,
> mollis et inculta sit mihi somnus humo.[79]

Herrick calls the country home an Elysium,[80] and his description of the dreams which rural life inspires may well have been suggested by Tibullus' description of the Elysian fields. Compare the following lines:

> The damask'd meadows and the pebbly streams
> Sweeten and make soft your dreams;
> The purling springs, groves, birds, and well weav'd bowers
> With fields enamelled with flowers,
> Present their shapes, while fantasy discloses
> Millions of lilies mix'd with roses.[81]

with Tibullus' conception of the Elysian fields:

> .... passimque vagantem
> dulce sonant tenui gutture carmen aves,
> fert casiam non culta seges, totosque per agros
> floret odoratis terra benigna rosis.[82]

Herrick's lines also suggest Propertius' description of the Golden Age:

> Felix agrestum quondam pacata iuventus
> divitiae quorum messis et arbor erant!....
> nunc violas tondere manu, nunc mixta referre
> lilia virgineos lucida per calathos,
> et portare suis vestitas frondibus uvas
> aut variam plumae versicoloris avem...
> altaque nativo creverat herba toro,
> pinus et incumbens laetas circumdabat umbras.[83]

---

[78]Tib. I, i, ll. 45-46.
[79]Tib. I, ii, ll. 73-74.
[80]"Thus let thy rural sanctuary be Elysium to thy wife and thee—" *A Country Life*, ll. 137-138.
[81]*A Country Life*, ll. 41-47.
[82]Tib. I, iii, ll. 59-63.
[83]Pro. III, xiii, ll. 25-26, 29-33, 36-37.

Herrick, like Horace and Tibullus, contrasts the peace of rural life with the cares of the merchant.

> Nor are thy daily and devout affairs
> Attended with those desp'rate cares
> Th' industrius merchant has, who for to find
> Gold, runneth to the Western Inde.[84]

Tibullus mentions the merchant:

> nec vagus ignotis repetens compendia terris
> presserat externa navita merce ratem:[85]

and, in another poem, having described an idyllic country life, he writes:

> hoc mihi contigat: sit dives iure, furorem
> qui maris et tristes ferre potest pluvias.[86]

There is in *A Country Life* yet another motif from Tibullus. Herrick affirms

> Wealth cannot make a life, but love.

Tibullus, in illustration of this idea, writes of a victorious and wealthy general:

> totus et argento contextus, totus et auro,
> insideat celeri conspiciendus equo;
> ipse boves mea si tecum modo Delia possim
> iungere et in solito pascere monte pecus,
> et te dum liceat teneris retinere lacertis,
> mollis et inculta sit mihi somnus humo.
> quid Tyrio recubare toro sine amore secundo
> prodest cum fletu nox vigilanda venit?[87]

Herrick's stress on the comfort, the pleasure even, of untroubled sleep was probably inspired by Tibullus. The idea appears recurringly in Herrick. The last lines of *The Country Life* (to Endymion Porter) are:

---

[84]*A Country Life,* ll. 63-67.
[85]Tib. I, iii, ll. 39-40.
[86]Tib. I, i, ll. 49-50.
[87]Tib. I, ii, ll. 69-76.

> O happy life! if that their good
> The husbandmen but understood
> Who all the day themselves do please
> And younglings, with such sports as these,
> And lying down, have nought t' affright
> Sweet sleep that makes more short the night.

Note also the lines already quoted:

> By whose warm side thou dost securely sleep
> While love the sentinel doth keep,
> With those deeds done by day which ne'er affright
> Thy silken slumbers in the night.[88]

Again, Herrick writes:

> Our peaceful slumbers in the night.[89]

In the same strain Tibullus had written:

> Divitias alius fulvo sibi congerat auro....
> Martia cui somnos classica pulsa fugent,
> me mea paupertas vita traducat inerti;[90]

and again:

> .... satis est requiescere lecto
> si licet et solito membra levare toro.
> quam iuvat immites ventos audire cubantem
> et dominam tenero continuisse sinu,
> aut gelidas hibernus aquas cum fuderit Auster
> securum somnos imbre iuvante sequi![91]

Herrick's line:

> "By whose warm side thou dost securely sleep"

is obviously based upon the last quoted of Tibullus' lines, and echoes it in diction as well as in content.

The Hock-Cart or Harvest Home, one of Herrick's best known poems on country life, not only describes customs strikingly like

---

[88]Herrick, *A Country Life: To his Brother.*
[89]Herrick, *His Content in the Country.*
[90]Tib. I, i, ll. 1 and 3-4.
[91]Tib. I, i, ll. 43-48.

those pictured by Tibullus, but at times probably borrows from the classical poets. The poem begins:

> Come, sons of summer, by whose toil
> We are the lords of wine and oil; ....
> Crown'd with the ears of corn, now come,
> And to the pipe sing Harvest Home!

Wine and oil, obviously, are not English crops, and Herrick in introducing them strikes at the very beginning of his poem a pseudo-classical note. The "ears of corn" in the next line are, of course, wheat ears—the traditional crown of the goddess Ceres.[92]

The poem continues with a description of the Devonshire Harvest Festival. This observance differs in details from the Roman celebrations, but the main elements are the same: thanksgiving and religious devotion, a white-robed procession, then the feast—eating, drinking, dancing, merriment. Excerpts from the poem are quoted below with elegiac parallels in the adjoining column.

THE WHITE PROCESSION

casta placent superis: pura cum
    veste venite
et manibus *puris* sumite fontis
    aquam.
cernite, *fulgentes* ut eat sacer agnus
    ad aras
vinctaque post olea *candida turba*
    comas.[93]

THE WHITE PROCESSION

Come forth, my lord, and see the cart
Dress'd up with all the country art.
See, here a maukin, there a sheet
As *spotless pure* as it is sweet;
The horses, mares, and frisking
    fillies
Clad all in linen *white as lilies*.[94]

DEVOTIONS

Quisquis adest, faveat: fruges
    lustramus et agros
ritus ut a prisco traditus extat
    avo.[95]

DEVOTIONS

Some bless the cart, some kiss the
    sheaves,
Some prank them up with oaken
    leaves;
Some cross the fill-house, some with
    great
Devotion stroke the home-borne
    wheat.

---

[92]See Tib. II, i. 1. 4: "spicis tempora cinge, Ceres;" and Ovid, *Amores* III, x, l. 3: "flava Ceres, tenues spicis redimita capillos."

[93]Tib. II, i, ll. 13-17.

[94]Note the stress of both the Latin and the English on cleanness and whiteness.

[95]Tib. II, i, ll. 1-3.

<table>
<tr><td>

THE OPEN FIRE

tunc nitidus plenis confisus rusticus
    agris
ingeret ardenti grandia ligna foco.[96]

</td><td>

THE OPEN FIRE

Well, on, brave boys, to your lord's
    hearth
Glitt'ring with fire.

</td></tr>
<tr><td>

THE FEAST

.... coronatus stabit et ipse calix.
at sibi quisque dapes et festas
    exstruet alte.[97]

</td><td>

THE FEAST

.... where, for your mirth
Ye shall see first the large and chief
Foundation of your feast, fat beef.

</td></tr>
<tr><td>

DRINKING

Nunc mihi fumosos veteris proferte
    Falernos
  consulis et Chio solvite vincla cado.
vina diem celebrent.[98]

</td><td>

DRINKING

And for to make the merry cheer,
If smirking wine be wanting here,
There's that which drowns all care,
    stout beer.

</td></tr>
<tr><td>

A HEALTH TO THE POET'S PATRON

sed 'bene Messallam' sua
  quisque ad pocula dicat.[100]

</td><td>

A HEALTH TO THE POET'S PATRON[99]

Which freely drink to your lord's
    health

</td></tr>
<tr><td>

CARE FOR THE OXEN

Solvite vincla iugis; nunc ad
    praesepia debent
  plena coronato stare boves
    capite.[101]

</td><td>

CARE FOR THE OXEN

Drink, frolic, boys, till all be blithe.
Feed and grow fat, and as ye eat
Be mindful that the lab'ring neat,
As you, may have their fill of meat.

</td></tr>
</table>

The last quoted lines of Tibullus influence one of Herrick's shorter poems on rural holidays, *Saint Distaff's Day, or The Morrow after Twelfth Day.*

<table>
<tr><td>

solvite vincla iugis, nunc ad
    praesepia debent
  plena coronato stare boves capite.
.... non audeat ulla
lanificam pensis imposuisse
    manum.[102]
    omnia sint operata deo.[103]

</td><td>

Partly work and partly play
Ye must on Saint Distaff's day;
From the plow soon free your team,
Then come home and fodder them;
If the maids a-spinning go,
Burn the flax and fire the tow;....
Give Saint Distaff all the right,
Then bid Christmas sport goodnight.

</td></tr>
</table>

---

[96]*Ibid.*, ll. 21-23.
[97]Tib. II, v, ll. 98-100.
[98]Tib. II, i, ll. 27-30.
[99]Mildmay, Earl of Westmorland, to whom the poem is addressed.
[100]Tib. II, i, l. 31.
[101]*Ibid.*, ll. 7-8.
[102]*Ibid.*, ll. 7-11.
[103]*Ibid.*, l. 9.

The parallel verses from Tibullus are in the adjoining column.

In several others of Herrick's bucolic poems influences of the Elegists may be traced. In *A New-Year's Gift to Sir Simeon Steward* occur the lines:

> Crackling laurel which foresounds
> A plenteous harvest to your grounds.

With this compare

> et succensa sacris crepitet bene laurea flammis,
> omine quo felix et sacer annus erit.[104]

In *The Poet Hath Lost his Pipe* Herrick writes

> My wearied oat I'll hang upon the tree
> And give it to the sylvan deities,

an echo of

> pendebatque vagi pastoris in arbore votum
> Garrula silvestri fistula sacra deo.[105]

In *A Pastoral to the King* Pan and Pales are mentioned in the same line:

> Fore-fend it Pan, and Pales do thou please
> To give an end.

The same two sylvan deities are linked by Tibullus:

> lacte madens illic suberat Pan ilicis umbrae
> et facta agresti lignea falce Pales.[106]

A Panegeric to Sir Lewis Pemberton contains the lines:

> .Thou has learnt thy train
> With heart and hand to entertain....
> As the old race of mankind did.....
> Thou do'st redeem these times; and what was lost
> Of ancient honesty may boast
> It keeps a growth in thee.

---

[104]Tib. II, v, ll. 81-82.
[105]*Ibid.*, ll. 29-30.
[106]*Ibid.*, ll. 27-28.

Tibullus expresses the same idea of "ancient honesty" in a description of the Golden Age:

> non domus ulla fores habuit, non fixus in agris,
> 　　qui regeret certis finibus arva lapis.[107]

In *His Age* Herrick writes of death:

> The pleasing wife, the house, the ground
> Must all be left, *no one plant found*
> 　　*To follow thee—*

an idea perhaps based on Tibullus' complaint:

> non seges est infra, non vinea culta.[108]

References to the Lares, the Genius or Birth-Spirit, and the "Household Gods" are commonplaces of Herrick's work.[109]

One group of Herrick's poems employs the phraseology of the Roman religious sacrifice. The following lines occur in *The Fairy Temple* or *Oberon's Chapel:*

> A little puppet-priest doth wait
> Who squeaks to all the comers there,
> 'Favor your tongues, who enter here.
> Pure hands bring hither without stain.'
> A second pules, 'Hence, hence, profane.'

It is particularly difficult to determine the source of such religious commonplaces.

> "Favor your tongues, who enter here"

may imitate Horace's "Favete linguis!"[110] but it is even more like Tibullus'

---

[107]Tib. I, iii, ll. 43-44.

[108]Tib. I, x, l. 35.

[109]Among his poems containing such references are: *To Sir John Berkley, To Anthea, The Invitation, To the King, Leprosy in Houses, To Lar, The Wassails, A Hymn to Sir Clipseby Crew, To his Worthy Friend, M. Thomas Falconbridge, The Primitiae to Parents, To his Household Gods, To his Closet-Gods, A Hymn to the Lares,* and *To the Genius of his House.*

[110]Horace, Od. III, i, l. 2.

quisquis ades, lingua, vir mulierque, fave,[111]

since "who enter here" is practically a translation of "quisquis ades." Again, "Hence, hence profane" may be a translation of Virgil's

Procul, O procul, este profani,[112]

but, on the other hand, the whole passage from Herrick may be based on Tibullus II, 1,—an elegy in the early part of which *all* the elements of the quoted lines appear, whereas neither Horace nor Virgil can be the model for the whole passage. Herrick's verses are quoted below with the parallels from Tibullus in the next column.

quisquis adest, faveat (sc. lingua)[113];	'Favor your tongues who enter here.
et *manibus puris* sumite fontis aquam.[114]	Pure hands bring hither without stain.'
vos quoque abesse procul iubeo.[115]	A second pules, 'Hence, hence, profane.'

Herrick was, of course, familiar with all three of the classical poets. He may have remembered, as he wrote, the verses of all three, may have taken one line from each. The phrase "pure hands," however, can have been borrowed only from Tibullus, and the other two motives are near at hand in the same elegy. Moreover, Herrick in another poem[116] links again two of the same elements:

Hence, hence, profane, soft silence let us have.

The last clause is a free rendering of "faveat lingua." This admonition properly means "Speak only words of good omen," but to the uninitiated it meant "Keep silence," since the "profane" could not be sure what words were ill omened. Again, it is only

---

[111]Tib. II, ii, 1. 2 (Grosart suggests this as Herrick's source).

[112]Virgil: *Aeneid* VI, 1. 258.

[113]Tib. II, i, 1. 1.

[114]*Ibid.*, 1. 14.

[115]*Ibid.*, 1. 11.

[116]Herrick, *A Dirge upon the Death of the Right Valiant Lord Bernard Stuart.*

in the elegy that both phrases occur together. In one other poem, *Another New Year's Gift, or Song for the Circumcision,* Herrick brings in the same theme:

> Hence, hence, profane, and none appear
> With anything unhallowed here.

This seems to be an echo of

> vos quoque abesse procul iubeo discedat ab aras
>   cui tulit hesterna gaudia nocte Venus.
> casta placent superis.[117]

Incense, a prominent feature of both Roman and Christian rites, is mentioned in *To His Saviour's Sepulcher* in a line which borrows from an elegy. Compare:

>   as from hence
> Flowed all Panchaia's frankincense
>   Rich Arabia did commix
> Here all her rare Aromatics,

with

> ....quas mittit dives Panchaia merces
> Eoique Arabes, dives et Assyria.[118]

Several others of Herrick's poems deal with sacrifices, but in so general a way that it seems unlikely that they had any definite sources. Among such poems are: *The Sacrifice,*[119] one of his poems *To Julia, A Hymn to the Muses, To Julia, the Flaminica Dialis or Queen-Priest, The Willow Garland,* and *The Entertainment or Porch-verse.*

As a final example of Herrick's treatment of Roman religious observances, note the parody on a classical prayer in the lines upon *Prudence Baldwin, her Sickness:*

> Prue, my dearest maid, is sick
> Almost to be lunatic.
> Aesculapius! come and bring

---

[117]Tib. II, i, ll. 11-13.

[118]Tib. III, ii, ll. 23-24.

[119]This poem is a good illustration of Herrick's tendency to mix Pagan with Christian or Hebrew elements.

> Means for her recovering.
> And a gallant cock shall be
> Offer'd up by her to thee.

The poet, as has been stated earlier in this chapter, addressed prayers to many of the Roman divinities.[120]   The subject of this particular prayer is especially characteristic of the Elegists.   Each of them wrote of the sickness of a mistress.[121]   In each case the poet made his elegy into a properly constructed Roman prayer consisting of *prex* (the request) plus *votum* (the promise of a reward to the god if he grants the suppliant's wish).   As an illustration, see the beginning and end of the elegy on *Sulpicia Sick:*

> Huc ades et tenerae morbas expelle puellae,
>   huc ades, intonsa Phoebe superbe coma.
>
> iam celeber, iam laetus eris, cum debita reddet
>   certatim sanctis gratus uterque focis.[122]

Observe that Herrick in his mock-supplication maintains the form of the Roman prayer.   The *prex* includes the first four lines of his stanza; the last two record his *votum*.

There remain for discussion, besides Herrick's love poems, a few miscellaneous lines showing influences of the Elegists.   In *Conubii Flores* Herrick refers to a Latin superstition cited by Ovid. Compare:

> vivit et armiferae cornix invisa Minervae
>   illa quidem saeclis vix moritura novem.[123]

with

> Live in the love of doves, and having told
> The raven's years, go hence more ripe than old.

In *So Music to Becalm a Sweet-sick Youth* the poet invokes

> Charms that call down the moon from out her sphere,

referring to a superstition mentioned by all the major Elegists. Compare with this line:

---

[120]See note 1.

[121]See Tib. III, v; III, x; III, xxvii; Pro. II, xxviii; II, xxviii a; Ovid, *Amores* II, xiii.

[122]Tib. IV, iv, ll. 1-3 and 21-22.

[123]Ovid, *Amores* II, vi, ll. 35-36.

> cantus et e curru Lunam deducere temptat;[124]

and

> audax cantatae leges imponere lunae.[125]

Herrick imitates Ovid's lines on twilight.
Compare:

> Twilight no other thing is, poets say,
> Than the last part of night and first of day,[126]

with

> qualia sublucent fugiente crepuscula Phoebe
> aut ubi nox abiit, nec tamen orta dies.[127]

Again, Ovid's complaint on too early dawn:

> optavi quotiens, aut ventus frangeret axem,
> aut caderet spissa nube retentus equus,[128]

probably inspired Herrick's lines:

> Time seems then not for to fly but creep;
> Slowly her chariot drives, as if that she
> Had broke her wheel, or crackt her axeltree.[129]

The discussion in the present chapter has been limited, in general, to Herrick's non-erotic verse. It is evident that the English poet was thoroly conversant with the work of all the Augustan Elegists. Influence of each individual, as well as traditions of the school as a whole, may be traced in Herrick's lines. As to the relative importance of the influence of the respective Elegists: one hundred thirty-four Latin parallels are cited in this chapter; of these seventy-three are from Tibullus, thirty-eight from Propertius, seventeen from Ovid, and six from Catullus. The heavy preponderance of the influence of the former poet is due to the

---

[124]Tib. I, viii, l. 21.
[125]Pro. IV, v, l. 13. See also Pro. II, xxviii, l. 37; and Ovid, *Amores* I, viii, l. 12.
[126]Herrick, *Twilight*.
[127]Ovid, *Amores* I, v, l. 5-7.
[128]Ovid, *Amores* I, xiii, ll. 29-30.
[129]Herrick, *To His Sweet Saviour*.

fondness of both Tibullus and Herrick for country life. A rather large proportion of Herrick's verse is on rural subjects, and it is natural that in this type of writing the one Elegist who particularly celebrates country life should have inspired the Devonshire poet's work. Herrick's erotic verse forms a class by itself, and will be treated in the next chapter.

CHAPTER IV

HERRICK'S LOVE POETRY

Among the Elegists it is Tibullus to whom Herrick's non-erotic verse is chiefly indebted, but in his amatory poetry the Englishman is influenced chiefly by Ovid. The tradition of writing poems to a mistress is old and widespread. Under courtly love it flourished as a well established medieval convention. In the Renaissance Platonic love was revived in a supposedly exalted strain, and a sonnet sequence to one's lady was a graceful tribute not to be omitted. In seventeenth century English verse both conventions are common. Samuel Daniel's *Sonnets to Delia* and Drayton's sonnets addressed to *Idea,* tho showing elegiac influence, are examples of the Renaissance pseudo-Platonic tradition rather than of the Latin erotic strain. Herrick's amatory verse, however, is distinctly Ovidian. Nothing in his lines suggests the reverence for womanhood, the exaltation of the loved one, that commonly characterized the songs of the Platonic love convention. Herrick expresses no desire for intellectual or spiritual communion with his mistresses. He delights in glowing, robust, physical charms. He is amorous as Ovid was amorous. Like Ovid he celebrates the advantages of variety, and boasts that he cannot possibly remain true to any one woman. His mistresses, like Ovid's Corinna, are either composite sketches of several women or entirely imaginary. Not one of them has a consistent personality—or, in fact, any distinct personality at all. He seldom even describes their physical beauty.[1] For the

---

[1]Only once does Herrick describe in detail the face of a mistress:

UPON HIS JULIA

Black and rolling is her eye,
Double chinn'd and forehead high;
Lips she has all ruby red,
Cheeks like cream enclareted;
And a nose that is the grace
And proscenium of her face.

This is distinctly realistic, and probably draws little inspiration from anything except its living model; thus tho

"Cheeks like cream enclareted"

sounds like a brunette version of "rose-leaves floated amid stainless milk," Propertius' description of Cynthia's complexion (Pro. II, III, 1. 12).

most part they are merely pretty Latinate names around which he weaves fanciful praises or descriptions of amorous experiences. His erotic complaints are often charming but never convincing. A good example is the poem *Upon the Loss of his Mistresses*.

> I have lost, and lately, these
> Many dainty mistresses:
> Stately Julia, prime of all;
> Sapho next, a principal;
> Smooth Anthea, for a skin
> White and heaven-like crystalline;
> Sweet Electra, and the choice
> Myrha, for the lute and voice;
> Next Corinna, for her wit,
> And the graceful use of it;
> With Perilla, all are gone,
> Only Herrick's left alone,
> For to number sorrow by
> Their departures hence, and die.

Not only is this plurality of mistresses reminiscent of Ovid, but the attributes of the girls are, for the most part, those ascribed by the Elegists to their sweethearts. Julia, *prima inter pares,* is "stately." Propertius' Cynthia was also stately, advancing with a walk worthy of the sister of Jove.[2] Of Sappho, the next of Herrick's *principiae,* no definite trait is recorded. Anthea, like Ovid's Corinna,[3] is lauded for the smoothness of her skin Electra is merely "sweet," but Myrha is noted, as was Propertius' mistress,[4] for her skillful playing and sweet voice. Corinna undoubtedly takes her name from Ovid's ladylove, and her wit and charm suggest Cynthia, the *docta puella.*[5]

[The poem in which Ovid boasts of his susceptibility to many loves strongly influenced Herrick, who based no less than four poems upon it. Its importance makes extended quotation advisable:[6]

---

[2]"incedit vel Jove digna soror" (Pro. II, II, 1. 6).
[3]"quam castigato planus sub pectore venter" (Ovid, *Amores* I, v, 1. 21).
[4]"et quantum Aeolio cum temptat carmina plectro
par Aganippeae ludere docta lyrae" (Pro. II, III, 11. 19-20).
[5]Pro. I, VII, 1. 11; II, XI, 1. 6; II, XIII, 1. 11.
[6]For the same theme in a less elaborated treatment, see Pro. II, XXII and XXV, 11. 40 *et seq.*

Non est certa meos quae forma invitet amores,
    centum sunt causae cur ego semper amem.
sive aliqua est oculos in se deiecta modestos,
    uror, et insidiae sunt pudor ille meae;
sive procax aliqua est, capior, quia rustica non est,
    spemque dat in molli mobilis esse toro.
aspera si visa est rigidasque imitata Sabinas,
    velle, sed ex alto dissimulare puto.

        . . . .

tu, quia tam longa es, veteres heroidas aequas
    et potes in toto multa iacere toro.
haec habilis brevitate sua est. corrumpor utraque;
    conveniunt voto longa brevisque meo.
non est culta—subit, quid cultae accedere possit;
    ornata est—dotes exhibet ipsa suas.
candida me capiet, capiet me flava puella,
    est etiam in fusco grata colore Venus.
seu pendent nivea pulli cervice capilli
    Leda fuit nigra conspicienda coma;
seu flavent, placuit croceis Aurora capillis.
    omnibus historiis se meus aptat amor.
me nova sollicitat, me tangit serior aetas;
    haec melior, specie corporis illa placet.
Denique quas tota quisquam probet urbe puellas,
    noster in has omnis ambitiosus amor.[7]

With this compare the following lines from Herrick:

LOVE DISLIKES NOTHING

Whatsoever thing I see,
Rich or poor although it be,
'Tis a mistress unto me.

Be my girl or fair or brown,
Does she smile or does she frown,
Still I write a sweet-heart down.

Be she rough or smooth of skin,
When I touch I then begin
For to let affection in.

Be she bold, or does she wear
Locks incurled of other hair,
I shall find enchantment there.

---

[7] Ovid, *Amores* II, IV, ll. 9-17 and 33 *ad finem*.

Be she whole or be she rent,
So my fancy be content,
She's to me most excellent.

Be she fat or be she lean,
Be she sluttish, be she clean,
I'm a man for every scene.

The same theme appears in *Love Lightly Pleased*.

Let fair or foul my mistress be,
Or low or tall, she pleaseth me.
Or let her walk or stand or sit,
The posture hers, I'm pleased with it.

Or let her tongue be still or stir,
Graceful is ev'rything from her.
Or let her grant or else deny,
My love will fit each history.

The last line is an exact translation of Ovid's

omnibus historiis se meus aptat amor.

In *Short and Long Both Likes,* Herrick condenses the theme into an epigram:

This lady's short, that mistress she is tall;
But long or short, I'm well content with all.

Still again he treats the subject, this time in an ugly burlesque:

No LOATHESOMENESS IN LOVE

What I fancy I approve,
No dislike there is in love;
Be my mistress short or tall,
And distorted therewithall;
Be she likewise one of those
That an acre hath of nose;
Be her forehead and her eyes
Full of incongruities;
Be her cheeks so shallow, too,
As to show her tongue wag through;
Be her lips ill hung or set
And her grinders black or jet;
Hath she thin hair, hath she none,
She's to me a paragon.

Herrick, like the Elegists, is interested in his mistress' clothes. In certain of his poems he appears definitely to imitate the Elegists' verses on the subject. The Augustans voiced three attitudes toward women's clothing: first, and most rarely, admiration and commendation; second—the most common attitude—reproof for too great extravagance; third, impatience that the clothes of a mistress should impede the lover's pleasure. Herrick writes in each of these three veins. His best known lines on the subject, *Upon Julia's Clothes,* are entirely complimentary.

> When as in silks my Julia goes,
> Then, then, methinks, how sweetly flows
> The liquefaction of her clothes.
>
> Next, when I cast mine eyes and see
> That brave vibration each way free,
> O how that glittering taketh me!

This suggests the lines from *Sulpicia's Garland:*

> illam, quidquid agit, quoquo vestigia movit,
> componit furtim subsequiturque Decor.
>   . . . .
> urit, seu Tyria voluit procedere palla;
> urit, seu nivea candida veste venit.[8]

The more usual elegiac attitude, reproof for extravagance and ostentation, is echoed in *Leprosy in Clothes.*

> When flowing garments I behold
> Enspired with purple, pearl, and gold,
> I think no other but I see
> In them a glorious leprosy.
>
>   . . . .
> As flow'rie vestures do descrie
> The wearer's rich immodestie;
> So plain and simple clothes do show
> Where virtue walks, not those that flow.

These lines are in the tradition of Propertius' admonition to Cynthia:

---

[8]Tib. III, viii, ll. 7-9 and 11-13.

> Quid iuvat ornato procedere, vita, capillo
> et tenues Coa veste movere sinus?
> aut quid Orontea crines perfundere murra,
> teque peregrinis vendere muneribus?[9]

The Elegist links virtue with simplicity by introducing the chaste
and unadorned beauties of Roman legend, then continues:

> Non illis studium vulgo conquirere amantes:
> illis ampla satis forma pudicitia.[10]

It is noteworthy that Herrick's standard for richness in dress—
"purple, pearl, and gold"—is not English but Roman, and may well
have been taken directly from the Elegists. Compare:

> illa gerat vestes tenues, quas femina Coa
> texuit, *auratas* disposuitque vias;....
> illi selectos certent praebere colores
> Africa puniceum *purpureumque Tyros*.[11]

and

> possideat ....
> ... quascumque niger rubro de litore gemmas
> proximus Eois colligit Indus aquis.[12]

In *Clothes Do but Cheat and Cosin Us* Herrick writes in the
vein of Ovid and Propertius, voicing the impatience of the lover
that his mistress' clothing should conceal her beauties from him.

> Away with silks, away with lawn;
> I'll have no screens or curtains drawn:
> Give me my mistress as she is,
> Drest in her nak't simplicities:
> For as my heart, e'en so mine eye
> Is won with flesh, not drapery.

Compare:

> Non iuvat in caeco Venerem corrumpere motu:
> si nescis, oculi sunt in amore duces....
> quod si pertendens animo vestita cubaris
> scissa veste meas experiere manus;[13]

---

[9]Pro. I, II, ll. 1 *et seq.*
[10]*Ibid.*, ll. 23-24.
[11]Tib. II, III, ll. 53-54 and 57-58.
[12]Tib. III, VIII, ll. 19-21.
[13]Pro. II, XV, ll. 11-12 and 17-18.

and

> crede mihi non ulla tuae est medicina figurae:
> nudus Amor formae non amat artificem.[14]

Ovid expresses the same attitude in the following account of a struggle with his mistress:

> Deripui tunicam—nec multum rara nocebat;
>   . . . .
> ut stetit ante oculos posito velamine nostros
> in toto nusquam corpore menda fuit.[15]

True to the elegiac tradition, most of Herrick's erotic verse is querulous in tone. Like the Augustans, he elaborates upon the sorrows of lovers in general, comments with due bitterness upon the perfidy of the fair, and particularly bewails his own hard fate. In *Not to Love,* he summarizes the traditional woes of the lover.

> There be in love as many fears
> As the summer's corn has ears:
> Sighs and sobs and sorrows more
> Than the sand that makes the shore:
> Freezing cold and fiery heats,
> Fainting swoons and deadly sweats:
>   . . . .
> Would'st thou know, besides all these,
> How hard a woman 'tis to please?
> How cross, how sullen, and how soon
> She shifts and changes like the moon;
> How false, how hollow she's in heart,
> And how she is her own least part;
> How high she's priz'd, and worth but small,
> Little thou'lt love or not at all.

This pessimistic effusion in its conceits and its piling up of parallels suggests the Petrarchan convention introduced into English by Wyatt and Surrey, but the theme and tone are in the tradition of Propertius. Compare the Elegist's warning to a friend who is trying to win Cynthia's favors:

---

[14]Pro. I, ɪɪ, ll. 7-8.
[15]Ovid, *Amores* I, v, ll. 13 and 17-18.

> quid tibi vis, insane?   meos sentire furores?
>   infelix, properas ultima nosse mala
> et miser ignotos vestigia ferre per ignes,
>   et bibere e tota toxica Thessalia.[16]

Even more dreadful are the pangs of love as described by Propertius in the following lines:

> tum magis Armenias cupies accedere tigres
>   et magis infernae vincula nosse rotae,
> quam pueri totiens arcum sentire medullis.[17]

Propertius, too, refers to love as a disease, tho he says it has no outward symptoms.   The victim walks abroad as usual—then suddenly his friends are bidden to his funeral.

> non eget hic medicis, non lectis mollibus aeger,
>   huic nullum caeli tempus et aura nocet;
> ambulat—et subito mirantur funus amici![18]

The work of the same Elegist offers plenty of models for Herrick's statement that women are always faithless:

> O nullis tutum credere blanditiis![19]

> formosis levitas semper amica fuit.[20]

> credule, nulla diu femina pondus habet.[21]

Herrick probably based on Propertius *His Misery in a Mistress*, in which he stresses his own unhappy plight:

> Happy you who can have seas
> For to quench you, or some ease
> From your kinder mistresses.
>
> I have one and she alone
> Of a thousand thousand known
> Dead to all compassion.

---

[16]Pro. I, v, ll. 3-6.
[17]Pro. I, ix, ll. 19-21.
[18]Pro. II, iv, ll. 11-13.
[19]Pro. I, xv, l. 42.
[20]Pro. II, xvi, l. 26.
[21]Pro. II, xxv, l. 22.

> Gentle friends, though I despair
> Of my cure, do you beware
> Of those girls which cruel are.

The same combination of ideas occurs in Propertius, tho in different order. It is too late for his own cure, the poet says. Let those rest at home in peace to whom love is kind. His own mistress is cruel. Let all lovers beware of such woes as he, the poet, endures.

> aut vos, qui sero lapsum revocatis, amici,
> quaerite non sani pectoris auxilia.

> vos remanete, quibus facili deus annuit aure,
> sitis et in tuto semper amore pares.
> in me nostra Venus noctes exercet amaras,
> et nullo vacuus tempore defit Amor.
> hoc, moneo, vitate malum.[22]

In *A Sonnet of Perilla,* Herrick echoes a frequent complaint of the Elegists:

> Then did I live when I did see
> Perilla smile on none but me.

The once favored lover has found himself supplanted by another. Compare:

> olim gratus eram: non illo tempore cuiquam
> contigit ut simili posset amare fide;[23]

and

> qui modo felices inter numerabar amantes,
> nunc in amore tuo cogor habere notam.[24]

Herrick follows the Elegists in writing of love as a wound which no remedies can heal:

> No herbs have power to cure love;
> Only one sovereign salve I know,
> And that is death, the end of woe.[25]

---

[22]Pro. I, i, ll. 25-26 and 31-35.
[23]Pro. I, xii, ll. 7-8.
[24]Pro. I, xviii, ll. 7-8.
[25]Herrick, *On Himself.*

and

> Some salve to every sore we may apply;
> Only for my wound there's no remedy.[26]

With these compare:

> omnes humanos sanat medicina dolores:
> solus amor morbi non amat artificem.[27]

> Quicquid erat medicae vicerat artis amor.[28]

> Non hic herba valet, non hic nocturna Cytaeis.
> non Perimedeae gramina cocta manus.[29]

In *The Dream* Herrick is more optimistic:

> Thus like a bee, Love, gentle still doth bring
> Honey to salve where he before did sting.

This suggests the classical idea of a wound's being cured by the weapon that inflicted it:

> Mysus et Haemonia iuvenis qua cuspide vulnus
> senserat, hac ipsa cuspide sensit opem.[30]

> Quid? non Haemonius, quem cuspide perculit, heros
> confossum medica post modo iuvit ope?[31]

Herrick's *To the Ladies* voices an attitude of Ovidian gallantry toward the fair:

> Trust me, Ladies, I will do
> Nothing to distemper you;
> If I any fret or vex,
> Men they shall be, not your sex.

In similar vein, Ovid had pledged immunity to women for all falsehoods and frailties:

---

[26]Herrick, *Upon Love*.
[27]Pro. II, i, ll. 57-58.
[28]Tib. II, iii, 1. 14.
[29]Pro. II, iv, ll. 7-8.
[30]Pro. II, i, ll. 63-64.
[31]Ovid, *Amores* II, ix, ll. 7-8.

> si deus ipse forem, numen sine fraude liceret
> femina mendaci falleret ore meum.[32]

Herrick, like the Elegists, regards love as a kind of warfare:

> Love is a kind of war. Hence those who fear!
> No cowards must his royal ensigns bear.[33]

Similarly Ovid writes:

> Militat omnis amans, et habet sua castra Cupido;
> Attice, crede mihi, militat omnis amans.[34]

The Elegists express contrasting opinions as to whether the active and zealous soldier or the man of peace is the better lover. In the *Amores,* Ovid inclines to the former view:

> Ergo desidiam quicumque vocabat amorem,
> desinat. ingenii est experientis amor.[35]

Propertius voices an opposing attitude:

> Pacis Amor deus est; pacem veneramur amantes.[36]

Herrick, with characteristic inconsistency, adopts both opinions. Compare:

> That man loves not who is not zealous, too;[37]

with

> The lazy man the most doth love.[38]

Propertius' epigrammatic summary of the limitations imposed by love upon the happiness of his votaries,

> nullus Amor cuiquam faciles ita praebuit alas
> ut non alterna presserit ille manu,[39]

---

[32]Ovid, *Amores* III, iii, ll. 43-44.
[33]Herrick, *On Love.*
[34]Ovid, *Amores* I, ix, ll. 1-2.
[35]*Ibid.,* ll. 31-32. See also *Amores* II, xii.
[36]Pro. III, v, l. 1.
[37]Herrick, *Zeal Required in Love.*
[38]Herrick, *Dissuasions from Idleness.*
[39]Pro. I, ix, ll. 23-24.

appears to have influenced Herrick in the following lines:

> God gives to none so absolute an ease
> As not to know or feel some grievances;[40]

and

> Fortune did never favor one
> Fully without exception;
> Though free she be, there's something yet
> Still wanting to her favorite.[41]

Herrick, like the Elegists, expresses in one breath the most pessimistic views on love, and in the next celebrates or pleads for its joys. He imitates in two poems[42] Catullus' *Vivamus mea Lesbia*,[43] the poet's plea for countless kisses, a lyric hendecasyllabic in metre, but in tone and theme closely allied to the erotic elegy.

> da mi basia mille, deinde centum,
> dein mille altera, dein secunda centum
> deinde usque altera mille, deinde centum.
> dein cum milia multa fecerimus,
> conturbabimus illa, ne sciamus
> aut nequis malus invidere possit,
> cum tantum sciat esse basiorum.[44]

Compare:

> Give me a kiss, add to that kiss a score,
> Then to that twenty add an hundred more;
> A thousand to that hundred: so kiss on
> To make that thousand up a million.
> Treble that million, and when that is done,
> Let's kiss afresh, as when we first begun.[45]

Herrick's *Kissing Usury* is based upon the same lines from Catullus.

In his lines *To Phillis,* Herrick writes:

---

[40]Herrick, *Ease.*
[41]Herrick, *Fortune's Favors.*
[42]Grosart's edition of Herrick notes this fact.
[43]Catullus, *Carmen* V.
[44]Catullus, *Carmen* V, ll. 7 *et seq.*
[45]*To Anthea.*

> Walk in the groves and thou shalt find
> The name of Phillis in the rind
> Of every straight and smooth-skin tree.

It would be impossible even to guess with any degree of probability the source of lines so conventional, but it is perhaps worth noting that a similar passage occurs in one of Propertius' elegies, and must have been familiar to Herrick.

> Vos eritis testes, si quos habet arbor amores,
>   fagus et Arcadio pinus amica deo.
> A quotiens teneras resonant mea verba sub umbras,
>   scribitur et vestris Cynthia corticibus.[46]

It would be equally impossible to determine positively the source of the following lines from *Tears are Tongues:*

> Tears are the noble language of the eye,
> And when true love of words is destitute,
> The eyes by tears speak while the tongue is mute;

but Ovid expressed the same idea in one line:

> Egit me lacrimis, ore silente, reum.[47]

Another case of the possible influence of Ovid occurs in the lines *To Oenone.*

> For shame or pity now incline
> To play a loving part;
> Either to send me kindly thine
> Or give me back my heart.

This suggests:

> quae me nuper praedata puella est
> aut amet aut faciat, cur ego semper amem.[48]

The Elegists frequently admonish their mistresses and friends on the danger of angering the gods by refusing to love. The man or woman who dares to resist Cupid or Venus is in danger of cruel punishment. Tibullus is particularly eloquent on the subject.[49]

---

[46]Pro. I, xviii, ll. 19-22.
[47]Ovid, *Amores* I, vii, l. 22.
[48]Ovid, *Amores* I, iii, ll. 1-2.

> Persequitur poenis tristia facta Venus,[50]

he writes, and again:

> oderunt, Pholoe, moneo, fastidia divi,[51]
> . . . .
> at te poena manet, ni desinis esse superba.[52]

In the same tradition are Herrick's lines *To Electra:*

> O beware! in time submit;
> Love has yet no wrathful fit.
> If her patience turns to ire,
> Love is then consuming fire.

The closest Latin elegiac parallel for this is:

> deus crudelius urit
> quos videt invitos succubuisse sibi.[53]

The course of love for the Elegists seems never to have run smooth. Most of their love poems are querulous. Others are defiant, warning the unfaithful or recalcitrant mistress that the poet has broken or is about to break the bonds that hold him. In this mood, Ovid writes:

> . . . . vitiis patientia victa est;
> cede fatigato pectore, turpis amor!
> scilicet adserui iam me fugique catenas;[54]

and Propertius:

---

[49]See also Pro. I, vii, ll. 25 and 26:
> "tu cave nostra tuo contemnas carmina fastu:
> saepe venit magno faenore tardus Amor."
and Ovid, *Amores* I, ii, ll. 17-19:
> "acrius invitos multoque ferocius urget
> quam qui servitium ferre fatentur Amor."
[50]Tib. I, viii, l. 28.
[51]*Ibid.*, l. 69.
[52]*Ibid.*, l. 77.
[53]Tib. I, viii, ll. 7-8.
[54]Ovid, *Amores* III, xi a, ll. 1-3.

> dabis mihi, perfida, poenas;
> et nobis aliquo, Cynthia, ventus erit.[55]

Herrick, true to tradition, also voices the conventional defiance:

> .... I'll devise
> Among the rest
> A way that's best
> How I may save mine eyes.[56]

Such outbursts of independence on the part of the Elegists were usually followed by a recantation.

> Valeatque Venus valeantque puellae,[57]

writes Tibullus, only to add ruefully:

> magna loquor, sed magnifice mihi magna locuto
> excutiunt clausae fortia verba fores.[58]

In the same mood Propertius writes:

> Liber eram et vacuo meditabar vivere lecto;
> at me composita pace fefellit Amor;[59]

and in another elegy:

> Et merito, quoniam potui fugisse puellam!
> nunc ego desertas alloquor alcyonas.[60]

Herrick, as usual, offers a contribution:

> HIS RECANTATION
>
> Love, I recant
> And pardon crave
> That lately I offended;
> But 'twas
> Alas
> To make a brave,
> But no disdain intended.

---

[55]Pro. II, v, ll. 3-4. See also Pro. III, xxiv.
[56]Herrick, *The Tear Sent to her from Stanes.*
[57]Tib. II, vi, l. 9.
[58]*Ibid.*, ll. 11-12.
[59]Pro. II, ii, ll. 1-2.
[60]Pro. I, xvii, ll. 1-2.

> No more I'll vaunt,
>   For now I see
> Thou only hast the power
>   To find
>   And bind
>   A heart that's free
> And slave it in an hour.

Tibullus, somewhat more seriously, expresses the same thought in two lines:

> Asper eram et bene discidium me ferre loquebar:
>   at mihi nunc longe gloria fortis abest.[61]

Expressions of devotion and loyalty to a mistress, common in the verse of the Elegists, find an occasional echo in Herrick's lines. In the verse *To Anthea Who May Command him Anything,* the Englishman writes:

> Thou art my life, my love, my heart,
>   The very eyes of me;
> And hast command of every part,
>   To live and die for thee.

This suggests Propertius' lines:

> Tu mihi sola domus, tu Cynthia, sola parentes,
>   omnia tu nostrae tempora laetitiae.[62]

One of Herrick's poems in which the influence of the Elegists is unusually obvious is *The Apparition of his Mistress Calling him to Elysium.*

> Let our souls fly to th' shades, where ever springs
> Sit smiling in the meads; where balm and oil,
> Roses and cassia, crown the untill'd soil.
>   . . . .
> Where every tree a wealthy issue bears
> Of fragrant apples, blushing plums or pears.
>   . . . .
> Here naked younglings, handsome striplings run
> Their goals for virgins' kisses which when done

---

[61]Tib. I, v, ll. 1-2.
[62]Pro. I, xi, ll. 23-24

> Then unto dancing forth the learned round
> Commix'd they meet, with endless roses crown'd.
> And here we'll sit on primrose banks, and see
> Love's chorus led by Cupid; ....
> There thou shalt hear divine Musaeus sing
> ....
> Then stately Virgil, witty Ovid, by
> Whom fair Corinna sits, and doth comply
> With ivory wrists his laureate head, and steeps
> His eye in dew of kisses while he sleeps;
> Then soft Catullus....

The title of this poem at once suggests Propertius, who in a well known elegy described the apparition of Cynthia.[63] The direct model, however, is the third elegy of Tibullus:[64]

> sed me, quod facilis tenero sum semper Amori
>   ipsa Venus campos ducet in Elysios.
> hic choreae cantusque vigent, passimque vagantes;
>   dulce sonant tenui guttere carmen aves;
> fert casiam non culta seges, totosque per agros
>   floret odoratis terra benigna rosis;
> ac iuvenum series teneris immixta puellis
>   ludit, et adsidue proelia miscet Amor.[65]

In the English poem Anacreon is described as "besmear'd with grapes." The quoted phrase was probably suggested to Herrick by his memory of a line from one of Tibullus' descriptions of a rural festival, in which the countryman is described as "oblitus musto."[66] Note that Herrick's poem—an excellent illustration of the extent to which its author borrowed and blended elements of Latin elegiac verse—directly imitates a passage from Tibullus, probably borrows its subject from Propertius, and refers by name to Ovid and Catullus, thus showing in the space of one poem the direct influence of all four of the Elegists.

A poem in which Latin influences are present but far less obvious is Herrick's *Welcome to Sack*. This sparkling, mock-heroic apostrophe, with its learned allusions to gods and heroes and famous beauties, its references to Roman religious rites, its extrava-

---

[63]Pro. IV, vii.
[64]This fact is noted by Judson in his *Seventeenth Century Lyrics*.
[65]Tib I, iii, ll. 57-64.
[66]Tib. II, v, l. 85.

gant endearments, and its coaxing reproaches, seems almost certainly a parody on the Latin love elegy. Tho it is a tissue woven of threads from many sources, it seems for the most part to echo Propertius, who, being at once the most impassioned and the most mannered of the Elegists, is the easiest to parody. The Alexandrian learning of the mythological and historical parallels, the exaggerated tributes to the charms of the mistress (here a vinous enchantress), the extravagance of the lover's protestations, all are Propertian. Moreover, certain lines may well be a parody on one definite elegy of Propertius. Selections from the English poem are quoted below with the suggested elegiac parallels in the adjoining column.

Cf. "mea vita"[67] and "mea lux,"[68] Propertius' endearing names for Cynthia.

> Soul of my life and fame!
> Eternal lamp of love! whose radiant flame
> Outglares the heav'ns' Osiris; and thy gleams
> Outshine the splendor of his midday beams.
> Welcome, O welcome, my illustrious spouse.
> Welcome as are the ends unto my vows.

nec sic errore exacto laetatus Ulixes,
   cum tetigit carae litora Dulichiae.[69]

> Ay, far more welcome than the happy soil
> The sea-scourg'd merchant, after all his toil,
> Salutes with tears of joy, when fires betray
> The smoky chimneys of his Ithica.
> . . . .

Unde tuos primum repetam mea Cynthia fastus?
   . . . .
quid tantum merui? quae te mihi carmina mutant?[70]
an quia parva domus mutato signa colore?
   et non ulla meo clamat in ore fides?[71]

> Why frowns my sweet? Why won't my saint confer
> Favors on me, her fierce idolater?
> . . . .
> Have I been cold to hug thee, too remiss
> Too temp'rate in embracing? . . . .

---

[67]Pro. I, II, l. 1; II, XXVI, l. 1.
[68]Pro. II, XXVII a, l. 59; II, XXIX, l. 1.
[69]Pro. II, XIV, ll. 3-4.
[70]Pro. I, XVIII, ll. 5 and 9.
[71]*Ibid.*, ll. 17-18.

an nova tristitiae causa puella
tuae?[72]

non est certa fides quam non in
iurgia vertas.[73]

....vasto labentur flumina ponto,
annus et inversas duxerit ante
vices
quam tua sub nostro mutetur
pectore cura.[74]

nunc mihi summa licet contingere
sidera plantis.[76]

omnia si dederis oscula, pauca
dabis.[77]
traicit et fati litora magnus amor.[78]

quod si forte aliqua nobis mutabere
culpa
vestibulum iaceam mortuus ante
tuum![80]

Have I divorced thee only to combine
In hot adult'ry with another wine?
True, I confess, I left thee, and
appeal
'Twas done by me more to confirm
my zeal
And double my affection on thee; as
do those
Whose love grows more enflamed by
being foes.
But to forsake thee ever, could
there be
A thought of such like possibility,
When thou thyself dar'st say thy
isles shall lack
Grapes before Herrick leaves Canary
sack?

Thou mak'st me airy, active to be
borne,
Like Iphyclus, upon the tops of corn.[75]
Thou mak'st me ....
.... ride the sunbeams.

Come, come and kiss me, love and
lust commends
Thee and thy beauties; kiss, we will
be friends
Too strong for fate to break us ....
.... come thou unto me
As Cleopatra came to Anthony.[79]
    ....
The time that I prevaricate from thee,
Call me the Son of Beer ....
....   let wine
Ne'er shine upon me, may my
numbers all
Run to a sudden death and funeral.

---

[72]*Ibid.,* 1. 10.

[73]Pro. III, VIII, 1. 19.

[74]Pro. I, xv, ll. 29-31. See also Pro. II, xv, ll. 31 *ad finem.*

[75]Both Propertius and Ovid allude to Iphyclus. See Pro. II, III, 1. 52, and Ovid's *Heroides* XIII, 1. 25.

[76]Pro. I, VIII a, 1. 43.

[77]Pro. II, xv, 1. 50.

[78]Pro. I, XIX, 1. 12.

[79]For an elegiac reference to Cleopatra, see Pro. III, XI, ll. 27 *et seq.*

[80]Pro. II, XIV, ll. 31-32.

The parallels quoted above are not to be interpreted as meaning that the present writer believes them to have been in every case the direct source of the lines with which they are compared. The real significance of the similarity of so many of Herrick's phrases to the Latin is the poet's great familiarity with the Elegists—particularly with Propertius, who is usually considered the least known of the group. A writer parodies only lines with which he is thoroly familiar. (One is reminded of Coleridge's use of the travel books and of similar material used in writing *The Ancient Mariner*.[81]) Propertius' verses must have arisen so spontaneously in Herrick's mind that they were the most natural form of expression for his mock love song. This ease and spontaneity furnish the *ne plus ultra* of evidence for Herrick's intimacy with the poetry of Propertius.

Herrick's diction and, to a less extent, his sentence structure were certainly influenced by the Latin poets. Any exhaustive study of such influences is beyond the scope of the present paper, but a few typical examples may well be noted. Herrick's trick of dividing a word at the end of a line is almost certainly borrowed from Catullus.[82] For example, the English poet writes:

> On then, and though you slow-
> ly go, yet howsoever go;[83]

> Treading upon vermillion and amber spice-
> ing the chaf'd air with fumes of Paradise;[84]

> The crown of duty is our duty: well-
> Doing's the fruit of doing well. Farewell;[85]

> Many a turn and man' a cross-
> Track, they redeem a bank of moss;[86]

> With eyes of peacocks' trains, and trout-
> Flies curious wings.[87]

---

[81]Lowes, J. L., *The Road to Xanadu*.
[82]Grosart, in his edition of Herrick, notes this fact.
[83]Herrick, *A Nuptial Song or Epithalamie on Sir Clipseby Crew and his Lady*, ll. 59 and 60.
[84]*Ibid.*, ll. 15 and 16.
[85]Herrick, *His Farewell unto Poetry*, ll. 103 and 104.
[86]Herrick, *Oberon's Palace*, ll. 25 and 26.
[87]*Ibid.*, ll. 68 and 69.

For examples of this usage in Catullus, see:

> Gallicum Rhenum horribilesque ulti-
> mosque Britannos;[88]

> quis deus magis est ama-
> tis petendus amantibus?[89]

> flere desine, non tibi, Au-
> runculeia, periculumst.[90]

Certain Latinate constructions recurringly appear in Herrick's verse. Chief among these is an absolute construction which seems to be the poet's rendering of the Latin ablative absolute. Examples chosen at random are:

> *Some few sands spent,* we hence must go;[91]
> *That done,* then wind me in that very sheet;[92]

> .... *which when done*
> Then unto dancing forth the learned round
> Commix'd they meet.[93]

Note particularly the last case cited, *which when done*. The use of the relative in an independent construction is clearly Latin. The phrase is undoubtedly Herrick's rendering of *quo facto*. Occasionally, also, in Herrick's use of tenses Latin influence may be perceived. An example is:

> When you shall see that I am dead,[94]

a clause in which English, less exact than Latin, would ordinarily use the present tense. The frequent elisions occurring in Herrick's verse may also be due to the poet's classical training.

No exact estimate of the proportion of romance to native words in Herrick's work is attempted here, but it is clear that his

---

[88]Catullus, XI, ll. 11-12.
[89]Catullus, LXI, ll. 46-47.
[90]*Ibid.,* ll. 86-87.
Wicks.
[91]Herrick, *A Paranoetical or Advisive Verse to his Friend, M. John*
[92]Herrick, *To Perilla.*
[93]Herrick, *The Apparition of his Mistress Calling him to Elysium.*
[94]Herrick, *The Cruel Maid.*

vocabulary is highly Latinate.   It is obvious, moreover, even to
the casual reader, that in many cases Herrick uses words in a Latin
rather than an English sense.[95]   Note, for example: *supremest*
(meaning *last*), *convinces* (*will conquer*), *retorted* (*drawn back*)
hairs, prime (*first* or *beginning*), *determines* (*ends, terminates*).
The words cited are Latinate in both sense and form.   In other
cases, Herrick literally translates Latin words or phrases.   His frequent use of *sweetly*—in such expressions, for instance as:

Come forth and *sweetly* die,[96]

is clearly a translation of the Latin *dulce*.   *Unshorn*, as an epithet
for Apollo, is, of course, *intonsus*.   *Black death* may well translate
Tibullus' *Mors atra,* and *golden pomp* is clearly Ovid's *aurea pompa*.   Moreover Herrick uses Latin prefixes with more than English
freedom.   He habitually coins such hybrids as *circum-walk, perpo-
lite, supervive, circumcrossed,* and many others.   Occasionally, also,
he joins an English prefix to a Latin root, as in *out-during*.

In general, it is evident that Herrick's borrowings from the
Elegists are both extensive and intensive.   Tho he seldom directly
imitates, his themes, his subjects, his moods and attitudes are those
of the Augustan Elegists.   Their phrases trip off his tongue so
naturally that to the casual reader there is no suggestion of Latin
influence.   He echoes, he varies, he parodies; and the resulting
verse usually seems entirely original and spontaneous.   Even his
Latinate constructions, so naturally does he use them, often suggest rather the whimsicality of the poet than the classical reading
which inspired them.   Herrick is, in a word, the seventeenth century's clearest exemplar of a foreign influence thoroly assimilated,
the final triumph of the Classical urge in the English Renaissance.

---

[95]In some cases of this usage he is, of course, merely following common
Renaissance custom.

[96]Herrick, *The Willow Garland.*

CONCLUSION

Not by chance did the erotic elegy of Alexandria and of Augustan Rome, quickening from its centuries of quiescence, take root in England in the sixteenth century, and in the seventeenth once more bear a copious harvest of amatory verse. Intellectually, politically, socially, England was a soil well fitted to nourish such a growth. The Renaissance of the sixteenth century effected in England what that earlier renaissance of the first and second centuries B.C. had effected in Rome. It raised interest in an older classical literature to such heights that soon all the literary world was gone after it; and of all the types of classical literature, none was easier to transplant to a new setting than the erotic elegy. Created by the cosmopolitan civilization of Alexandria, perfected by the urban culture of Rome, it was one of the most universal of literary types. Caring nothing for political, social, or ethical ideals, it lacked the narrowness of a purely national expression: its interests were those of the individual—subjective, hence universal and perennial.

In the normal development of the Renaissance, moreover, the influences of the classical elegy naturally culminated in the seventeenth century. Thruout the sixteenth, the tide of classical literature had flowed into England. First the new models were edited, then translated, then freely imitated; and at last, during the reign of Elizabeth, they were quite assimilated to the native literary traditions. True, the elegies did not pass thru all the stages of this orderly transition, for the censorship of the conservative ecclesiastical authorities had prevented the translation of the licentious Augustan love lyrics[1] (tho not their influence, since the poets might read them in the original). The paganism of Italy, however, gradually permeating England, eventually brought in a new literary freedom, and, thus, seventeenth century love lyrics, far from the decorum of eighteenth century poetry, might approach the Augustans themselves in frankness and cynicism.

---

[1] The only one of the Elegists whose works were translated prior to 1600 was Ovid, and the only complete translation of his poems (by Christopher Marlowe, c. 1598) was publicly burned by order of the Bishop of London and the Archbishop of Canterbury.

"Body differs not more from soul," writes Francis Thompson, "than the Amor of Catullus or Ovid differs from the love of Dante or Shelley."[2]   The comparison is valid for the thirteenth century and for the nineteenth, but the love poems of the seventeenth are much more closely akin to those of the first century B.C. than to the Platonic idealism of either the late Middle Ages or of the Romantic Movement.

The political and social conditions of the seventeenth century were also conducive to the popularity of the love elegy. With the Spanish menace removed by the destruction of the Armada in 1588, the throbbing patriotism of the age of Elizabeth began to subside, and by the end of the century personal rather than national interests once more dominated the minds of Englishmen. The Renaissance urge toward individualism was strong, and individualism brings with it subjectivity. The opposing Renaissance element, love for and imitation of the classics, was still dominant. In this conflict of forces, once again, as in the days of Augustan Rome, the erotic elegy offered itself as a nicely balanced combination: in form, a classical literary type of great antiquity; in content, a vehicle for the most subjective of human passions. The conditions of literary production, too, were those conducive to the writing of a body of erotic verse, were in fact not unlike those of Alexandria and of Augustan Rome. Once more the political, social, and literary center of a nation was a single great city in which the court was the center of both literary patronage and of social life. Once more poets were, for the most part, learned men, and learned men poets of a sort, for the non-dramatic poetry of the seventeenth century, like that of Alexandria and Rome, was written chiefly by and for the upper classes. Once more women, many of whom were more noted for beauty than for chastity, were socially prominent, and love intrigues were common. In such an atmosphere erotic verse has always flourished.

Ovid was the particular idol of the seventeenth century lyrists, and the reason is not far to seek: he took love lightly, bragged of it, mocked it. His very lack of seriousness, his grace and facility, his carefree mockery, endeared him to Englishmen to whom love was a game, and love poetry a convention. The English poets lacked, as Ovid had lacked, the sincerity and tenderness of Tibullus

---

[2]Francis Thompson, *Paganism Old and New.*

and Propertius at their best. Like Ovid, the cavaliers demanded of their mistresses only beauty and "kindness," and offered in return, not spiritual devotion, but graceful, often cynical wreaths of song. True, the works of Tibullus and Propertius are themselves conventional, but it is impossible not to feel at times the sincerity of the poet transmuting the traditional *querimonium* into a poignant and personal thing, the expression of an elemental longing that shines clearly through the artificiality of the ancient poetic form.

The exact influence of the elegies is somewhat difficult to define. The elegiac metre was not much used in English, tho a few poets did attempt it—notably Campion, who employed it for epigrams. Since the Latin elegy had no fixed plan and varied greatly in length, it could set no standard as to arrangement of content. Its influences were, then, not on form but on content, and may be divided into two phases: the influence of specific passages of poems and the less definite but more pervasive effect of the Latin erotic tradition with its frank but elegant animalism, its combination of grace and artificiality with elemental passion—a tradition that blended with and at times superseded the Platonic and courtly love conventions that had dominated the erotic verse of the preceding century. In short, the elegiac revival under the Stuarts seems to be the last free flowering of the Renaissance, the final phase of the free assimilation and adaptation of the classics begun, in England, in the sixteeneth century; and with its contrasting yet fusing elements of primitive licentiousness and artificial refinement, it forms the logical transition from the courtly and Platonic love conventions to the refined immorality of the Restoration.

BIBLIOGRAHY

Roman Poets

Catullus, *Carmina*, D. C. Heath and Company, Boston, 1924.

Ovid, *Heroides* and *Amores*, William Heinemann, London, 1925.

Propertius, *Opera*, William Heinemann, London, 1924.

Tibullus, *Opera*, in *Catullus, Tibullus, and Pervigilium Veneris*, William Heinemann, London, 1925.

Horace, *Odes and Epodes*, Ginn and Company, Boston, cp. 1903.

Virgil, *The Eclogues, Georgics and Moretum*, Eldridge and Brother, Philadelphia, 1872.

English Poets

Beaumont, Francis, *Poems*, in Chalmers, Alexander, *The Works of the English Poets*, Vol. VI, London, 1810.

Beaumont, Sir John, *Poems*, in Chalmers, Alexander, *The Works of the English Poets*, Vol. VI, London, 1810.

Brown, Alexander, *Poems*, in Chalmers, Alexander, *The Works of the English Poets*, Vol. VI, London, 1810.

Campion, Thomas, *Works*, Clarendon Press, Oxford, 1909.

Carew, Thomas, *Poems*, printed for the Roxbridge Library, London, 1870.

Cowley, Abraham, *Poems*, Cambridge University Press, 1905.

Crashaw, Richard, *Poems, English, Latin, and Greek*, Clarendon Press, Oxford, 1927.

Donne, John, *Complete Poems*, Robson and Sons, London, 1872-73.

Drayton, Michael, *Poetical Works*, Mundell and Son, Edinburgh, 1793.

Fletcher, Giles and Phineas, *Poetical Works*, Cambridge University Press, 1908.

Herrick, Robert, *Complete Poems*, Robson and Sons, London, 1876.

Jonson, Ben, *Poetical Works*, Mundell and Son, Edinburgh, 1793.

Lovelace, Richard, *Poems*, Clarendon Press, Oxford, 1925.

Suckling, Sir John, *Poetical Works*, Mundell and Son, Edinburgh, 1793.

Waller, Edmund, *Poems*, Lawrence and Bullen, London, 1893.

Reference Works

Breasted, James Henry, *Ancient Times*, Ginn and Company, Boston, 1916.

Carter, Jesse Benedict, *Selections from the Roman Elegiac Poets*, D. C. Heath and Company, Boston, cp. 1900.

Croiset, Alfred and Maurice, *Abridged History of Greek Literature*.

Duff, J. Wight, *A Literary History of Rome*, T. F. Unwin, London, 1909.

Ellis, Robinson, *Catullus in the Fourteenth Century*, Oxford, 1905.

Commentary on Catullus, Clarendon Press, Oxford,[2] 1889.

Harrington, K. P., *Catullus and his Influences,* Marshall Jones Company, Boston, 1923.

Judson, A. C., *Seventeenth Century Lyrics,* University of Chicago Press, 1927.

Rand, E. K., *Ovid and his Influences,* Marshall Jones Company, Boston, 1925.

Sandys, Sir J. E., *History of Classical Scholarship,* Cambridge University Press, 1908.

Schanz, Martin, *Geschicte der Römischen Litteratur bis zum Gesetzgebungswerk des Kaisers Justinian,* München, 1911.

Schulze, K. P., *Römische Elegiker, Eine Auswahl aus Catull, Tibull, Properz, und Ovid,* Weidmannsche Buchhandlung, Berlin, 1900.

Sellar, W. Y., *The Roman Poets of the Augustan Age,* Clarendon Press, Oxford, 1892.

Smith, Kirby Flower, *The Elegies of Albius Tibullus,* American Book Company, New York, 1913.

Illustrations on Tibullus, American Journal of Philology, XLIII.

INDEX

Aeditus, Valerius, 17
Alexander of Aetolia, 15
Anacreon, 100
Antimachus of Colophon, 13
Archilochus of Paros, 12

Bangor Public Lbrary, 5
Beaumont, Francis, 33-34
  Charm, 33
  *Masque of the Gentlemen of Gray's
    Inn and the Inner Temple, A,* 34
Beaumont, Sir John, 33, 34
Breasted, James Henry, *Ancient
  Times,* 14n
Bullen, A. H., 43n

Callimachus, 15-16, 18
Callinus of Ephesus, 12
Campion, Thomas, 43-44, 108
  Leave Prolonging thy Distress, 44
  "O Love, where are thy shafts," 44
  "Shall I come, sweet Love, to
    thee," 44
  Song, 43
  There is None O None but You, 43
  Translation of Catullus, *Carmen V,*
    44
Carew, Thomas, 34-35, 44-46
  *An Elegie upon the Death of Dr.
    Donne, Dean of Paul's,* 35
  Love's Force, 46
  Persuasions to Jóy, 46
  Persuasions to Love, 44-45, 46
  Song, 46
  Spark, The, 46
  Tinder, The, 46
  *To his Mistress Retiring in
    Affection,* 46
  To his Unconstant Mistress, 45
  To My Inconstant Mistress, 46
  Ungrateful Beauty Threatened, 45
Carter, Jesse Benedict, *Selections
  from the Roman Elegiac Poets,*
  21n, 25n
Catullus, Carm. II a, 39
    "   V, 19, 56n, 68, 95
    "   VIII, 20, 44
    "   XI, 104
    "   XIII, 42, 51
    "   XVI, 55
    "   XXVII, 20
    "   XLV, 42
    "   XLVIII, 42
    "   LXI, 104
    "   LXVIII, 68

Catullus, Carm. LXVIII a, 69
    "   LXX, 42
    "   LXXII, 42
    "   LXXV, 42
    "   LXXXII, 42
    "   LXXXVI, 42
    "   LXXXVII, 42
Catullus, Quintus, 17
Chase, Dean George Davis, 5
Chaucer, Geoffrey, 27, 51
Coleridge, Samuel Taylor, quoted,
  12, 103
Cowley, Abraham, 9, 36-38
  Complaint, The, 38
  Cure, The, 38
  Epigram on the Power of Love, 37
  Given Love, 38
  Inconstant, The, 37
  Monopoly, The, 38
  Ode from Catullus, 38
  *Ode upon Occasion of a Copy of
    Verses of My Lord Broghell's,*
    37
  Request, The, 37
  Vain Love, 38
  Waiting Maid, 38
Crawshaw, Richard, 36
Croiset, Alfred and Maurice,
  *Abridged History of Greek Lit-
    erature,* 11n, 12n, 13n, 15n

Daniel, Samuel, 9, 27, 28, 31-32, 84
  Sonnets to Delia, 31 & notes, 32
Dante Alighieri, 107
Donne, John, 27, 34 & n, 35 & n, 36,
  42n
  Indifferent, The, 35
  Sun Rising, The, 35n
Draper, John W., 5
Drayton, Michael, 27-31, 84
  Idea, 28, 29, 30, 31
  Idea's Mirror, 28, 29, 30
  Muses' Elysium, The, 31
  Ode to the New Year, 30 & n
  Quest of Cynthia, The, 31
  Shepherd's Garland, The, 30 & n
  Shepherd's Sirena, The, 30 & n
  To his Rival, 28
Duff, J. W., 10 & n, quoted, 14
  A Literary History of Rome,
    10 & n, 14n, 16n, 17n, 18n, 19n,
    20n, 23n, 25n

Ellis, Milton, 5

Ellis, Robinson, 9 & n
  Catullus in the Fourteenth Century, 9n
  Commentary on Catullus, 9n
  Prolegomena, 9n
Ennius, 17
Euphorion, 18

Fletcher, John, *To the Author,* by
  J. F., 34
Fletcher, Phineas, 32-33
  Piscatory Eclogues, 32, 33

Gallus, 16, 18
Grosart, A. B., edition of Herrick,
  79, 95n, 103n

Hale, Edward Everett, Jr., comments
  upon Herrick in his *Selections
  from the Poetry of Robert
  Herrick,* 51n
Harper's *Dictionary of Classical
  Literature and Antiquities,* 11n
Harrington, K. P., 9 & n
  Catullus and His Influence, 9 & n
Hawkins, Thomas, *An Elegy Dedi-
  cated to the Memory of Sir John
  Beaumont,* 33 & n
Hermesianax of Colophon, 15
Herrick, Robert, 5, 9, 10, 27, 38,
  46-105
  Another Ceremony, 70n
  *Another New Year's Gift, or Song
  for the Circumcision,* 80
  Another to Neptune, 48n
  *Apparition of his Mistress Calling
  him to Elysium, The,* 99-100, 104
  Best to be Merry, 61
  Canticle to Bacchus, 48n
  *Ceremonies for Candlemas Day,
  The,* 70n
  Ceremonies for Candlemas Eve,
  70n
  Ceremonies for Christmas, 70n
  Ceremony upon Candlemas Eve,
  70n
  Christmas Eve, 70n
  *Clothes Do but Cheat and Cosin
  Us,* 89
  Conubii Flores, 81
  Corinna's Going A-Maying, 62, 70n
  Country Life, The, 69-70
  Country Life, The, (to Endymion
  Porter), 70-71n, 73-74
  *Country Life: To his Brother, Mr.
  Thomas Herrick, A,* 70n, 71-73
  Cruel Maid, The, 58, 67, 104
  Departure of the Good Demon, 48n

*Dirge upon the Death of the Right
  Valiant Lord Bernard Stuart, A,*
  79n
Dissuasions from Idleness, 94
Dream, The, 93
Ease, 95
End Decreed, An, 61
*Entertainment or Porch-Verse,
  The,* 80
*Fairy Temple, or Oberon's Chapel,
  The,* 78
Fortune's Favors, 95
Hesperides, 52
His Age, 61, 78
His Charge to Julia at his Death,
  64
His Content in the Country, 70n, 74
His Embalming to Julia, 65
His Farewell unto Poetry, 103
His Misery in a Mistress, 91
His Poetry His Pillar, 52
His Recantation, 98-99
His Return to London, 68
Hock-cart or Harvest Home, The,
  70n, 74-76
Hymn to Cupid, A, 48n
Hymn to Juno, A, 48n
Hymn to Sir Clipseby Crew, A,
  78n
Hymn to the Lares, A, 78n
Hymn to the Muses, A, 48n, 80
Invitation, The, 78n
Kissing Usury, 95
Lar's Portion and the Poet's Part,
  48n
Leprosy in Clothes, 88
Leprosy in Houses, 78n
Love Dislikes Nothing, 86-87
Love Lightly Pleased, 87
Lyric to Mirth, A, 60, 61
Maypole, The, 70n
Meditation for his Mistress, A,
  57-58
Mount of the Muses, The, 53-54
*New Year's Gift to Sir Simeon
  Steward, A,* 70n, 77
No Loathesomeness in Love, 87
Not to Love, 90
*Nuptial Song or Epithalamie on
  Sir Clipseby Crew and his Lady,
  A,* 103
Oberon's Palace, 103
*Ode to Master Endymion Porter
  upon his Brother's Death,* 68
On Himself, 53, 54, 92
On Love, 94
*Panegyric to Sir Lewis Pember-
  ton, A,* 77

Herrick, Robert—(Continued)
*Paranoeticall or Advisive Verse to
his Friend, Mr. John Wicks, A,*
59, 104
Pastoral to the King, A, 77
Pillar of Fame, The, 52n, 54-55
Poet Hath Lost his Pipe, The, 77
Poets, 55
Primitiae to Parents, The, 78n
Prudence Baldwin, her Sickness,
80-81
Request to the Graces, A, 48n
Sacrifice, The, 80
Saint Distaff's Day, 70n, 76-77
Short and Long Both Likes, 87
Short Hymn to Lar, A, 48n
Short Hymn to Venus, 48n
*So Music to Becalm a Sweet-sick
Youth,* 81
Sonnet to Perilla, A, 92
Sulpicia's Garland, 88
Sulpicia Sick, 81
Tears are Tongues, 96
Tear Sent to her from Stanes, The,
98
To a Bed of Tulips, 59
To Anthea, 66, 78n, 95
*To Anthea Who May Command
him Anything,* 99
To Daffodils, 59
To Electra, 61, 97
To Enjoy the Time, 61
To his Closet-Gods, 48n, 78n
*To his Dying Brother, Master
William Herrick,* 68
To his Household Gods, 48n, 78n
To His Lovely Mistresses, 65
To His Muse, 48n
To His Saviour's Sepulcher, 80
To His Sweet Saviour, 82
*To his Worthy Friend, M. Thomas
Falconbridge,* 78n
To Julia, 68, 80
*To Julia, the Flaminica Dialis or
Queen-Priest,* 80
To Lar, 48n, 78n
To Laurels, 67
To Live Freely, 61, 62
*To Live Merrily and Trust to
Good Verses,* 50-51
To Myrrha Hard-hearted, 59
To Oenone, 96
To Perilla, 63-64, 68, 104
To Phillis, 95
To Sappho, 61
To Sir John Berkley, 78n
To the Genius of his House, 78n
To the King, 78n
To the Ladies, 93

*To the Reverend Shade of his
Religious Father,* 65
To the Virgins, 56-57
To Youth, 61
Twelfth Night, 70n
Twilight, 82
Upon Himself, 53, 54, 92
Upon his Julia, 84n
Upon Julia's Clothes, 88
Upon Love, 93
Upon the Loss of his Mistresses, 85
Vow to Mars, A, 48n
Vow to Minerva, A, 48n
Wake, The, 70n
Wassails, The, 78n
Welcome to Sack, 100-103
Willow Garland, The, 80, 105
Zeal Required in Love, 94
Hesiod, 16
Homer, 16, 51n
Horace, Carm. I, xi, 31
　　　" 　 III, i, 78
　　　" 　 III, xxx, 52, 53, 55

Jonson, Ben, 27, 34n, 38-40, 42n
Elegy, An, 39
His Discourse with Cupid, 39
Ode, An, 39
Ode to Himself, 39
*Sonnet to the Noble Lady, the
Lady Mary Wroth, A,* 39
Judson, A. C., 10 & n
Seventeenth Century Lyrics,
10 & n, 100n

Lovelace, Richard, 42-43
Love Inthroned, 42
Love Made in the First Age, 42
On Sanazar's Being Honored, 42
Lowes, J. L., *The Road to Xanadu,*
103n
Lucilius, 17
Lygdamus, 63n
Marinism, 27, 55
Marlowe, Christopher, translation of
Ovid, 106n
Menander, 16
Mimnermus of Colophon, 13
Moorman, F. W., in *The Cambridge
History of English Literature,* 10

Ovid, *Amores* I, i, 33
　　　" 　 I, ii, 30n, 31, 38, 40
　　　" 　 I, iii, 25, 43, 52, 96
　　　" 　 I, iv, 25
　　　" 　 I, v, 82, 85n, 90
　　　" 　 I, vi, 44
　　　" 　 I, vii, 96
　　　" 　 I, viii, 25, 41n, 82

Ovid, *Amores*—(Continued)
"   I, ix, 94
"   I, xi, 31, 42
"   I, xiii, 35n, 82
"   I, xv, 16n, 30, 52, 53,
    54, 55
"   II, i, 30, 30n
"   II, ii, 26
"   II, iii, 26
"   II, iv, 26, 35, 46, 47, 86
"   II, v, 37
"   II, vi, 81
"   II, vii, 25, 38
"   II, viii, 25
"   II, ix, 28, 42, 44, 52, 93
"   II, x, 26, 33
"   II, xii, 94
"   II, xiii, 81
"   II, xvi, 31, 33
"   II, xix, 26, 36, 41
"   III, iii, 31, 38, 94
"   III, iv, 34
"   III, ix, 31n, 52, 53
"   III, x, 70, 75
"   III, xi, 46
"   III, xi a, 97
"   III, xiii, 70
"   III, xxi a, 20
"   III, xxiv, 45
Heroides xiii, 102
Rem. Am., 37

Parthenius of Nicea, 16
Phanocles, 15
Philetas, 15, 16, 18
Phocylides of Miletus, 13
Postgate, J. P., *Catullus, Tibullus,
   and Pervigilium Veneris*, 29n
Praz, Mario, *Secentismo e Marinis-
   mo in Inghilterra*, 27n
Propertius, I, i, 38, 41, 92
"   I, ii, 89, 90, 101
"   I, v, 91
"   I, vii, 30, 85
"   I, viii a, 25, 102
"   I, ix, 91, 95
"   I, xi, 99
"   I, xii, 92
"   I, xiv, 19, 30
"   I, xv, 24, 91, 102
"   I, xvi, 31, 44, 64
"   I, xvii, 33n, 63, 98
"   I, xviii, 92, 96, 101, 102
"   I, xix, 24, 56, 102
"   II, i, 32, 38, 43, 44, 67, 93
"   II, ii, 23, 85n, 98
"   II, iii, 23, 31, 39n, 40,
    84n, 85n, 102
"   II, iv, 33n, 91, 93

"   II, v, 20, 24, 29, 36, 46, 98
"   II, viii, 24
"   II, viii a, 24
"   II, ix, 33
"   II, xi, 85
"   II, xii, 24
"   II, xiii, 85
"   II, xiii a, 63, 64, 65, 66,
    67
"   II, xiv, 101, 102
"   II, xv, 19, 56, 57, 59, 60,
    62, 90, 102
"   II, xvi, 91
"   II, xix, 71
"   II, xxi, 36
"   II, xxii, 85
"   II, xxiv a, 32
"   II, xxv, 29, 85, 91
"   II, xxvi, 101
"   II, xxvii a, 101
"   II, xxviii, 43, 81, 82
"   II, xxviii a, 58, 61, 81
"   II, xxix, 101
"   II, xxx, 52
"   II, xxxiii, 20
"   II, xxxiv, 70
"   III, i, 30n, 52, 54
"   III, ii, 52
"   III, iii, 30n
"   III, v, 94
"   III, viii, 102
"   III, xi, 102n
"   III, xiii, 31n, 72
"   III, xvi, 63, 66
"   III, xviii, 30
"   III, xxiv, 45
"   III, xxv, 56, 60
"   IV, i, 22
"   IV, v, 41n, 82
"   IV, vi, 70
"   IV, vii, 63, 64, 66, 100
"   IV, viii, 24

Quintilian, 16, 18

Rand, E. K., *Ovid and His Influence*,
   10 & n
Rowe, Nicholas, 9

Sandys, John Edwin, *History of
   Classical Scholarship*, 15n
Schanz, Martin, *Geschichte der
   Römischen Litteratur bis zum
   Gesetzgebungswerk des Kaisers
   Justinian*, 11n, 13n, 15n, 16n
Schiller, J. C. F., 12 & n
   Gedichte, "Das Distichon,"
   quoted, 12n

Schulze, K. P., *Römische Elegiker, Eine Auswahl aus Catull, Tibull, Propers, und Ovid,* 11n, 12n, 13n, 16n
Sellar, W. J., *The Roman Poets of the Augustan Age,* quoted, 14-15, 15n, 16n, 17n, 18n
Shelley, Percy Bysshe, 107
Simonides of Ceos, 13
Smith, Kirby Flower, 9 & n
    The Works of Albius Tibullus, 9 & n
    Illustrations on Tibullus, 9 & n
Solon of Athens, 13
Sophocles, 16
Spenser, Edmund, 27, 28
Suckling, Sir John, 36
    Love Turned to Hatred, 36
    Upon A. M., 36
Surrey, Earl of, Henry Howard, 90

Theocritus, 18
Theognis of Megara, 13
Thompson, Francis, *Paganism Old and New,* 107
Tibullus, I, i, 19, 21, 31, 56, 57, 60, 62, 63, 69, 70, 71, 72, 73, 74
    " I, ii, 22, 34, 41n, 71, 72, 73
    " I, iii, 22, 30n, 40, 63, 69, 72, 73, 78, 100
    " I, iv, 19, 38, 52, 56, 57, 58, 62
    " I, v, 21, 29, 32, 42, 71, 99
    " I, viii, 32, 33, 41n, 56, 57, 60, 61, 82, 97
    " I, x, 22, 70, 71, 78
    " II, i, 21, 70, 75, 76, 79, 80
    " II, ii, 70, 79
    " II, iii, 31n, 33n, 37, 89, 93

    " II, iv, 38
    " II, v, 32, 70, 76, 77, 100
    " II, vi, 98
    " III, ii, 44, 63, 64, 65, 67, 80
    " III, iv, 38
    " III, v, 81
    " III, vi, 20
    " III, viii, 88, 89
    " III, x, 81
    " III, xxvii, 81
    " IV, iv, 81
Tyrtaeus, 12

Vergil, Aen. VI, 79
Vivian, S. P., edition of Campion's Works, 43n

Waller, Edmund, 40-42
    Apology of Sleep, The, 41
    Countess of Carlisle, The, 41
    Go, Lovely Rose, 42
    Of Divine Love, 40
    Servant to Sacharissa, 42
    Song, A, 40
    To a Friend of the Different Success of their Loves, 41
    To a Lady in Retirement, 42
    To Mrs. Braughton, 42
    To Phyllis, 42
    To the Mutable Fair, 41-42
Walsh, William, 9
Watt, Robert, *Bibliotheca Britannica,* 27n
Widener Library, 5
Wyatt, Sir Thomas, 90

Xenophanes of Colophon, 13